T0369233

UNFINISHED JOURNEY
From War to Peace
From Violence to Wholeness

Jerry Pedersen

Order this book online at www.trafford.com
or email orders@trafford.com

Most Trafford titles are also available at major online book retailers.

Note for Librarians: A cataloguing record for this book is available from Library
and Archives Canada at www.collectionscanada.ca/amicus/index-e.html

Printed in Victoria, BC, Canada.

ISBN: 978-1-4269-0402-8 (sc)
ISBN: 978-1-4269-0404-2 (eb)

Library of Congress Control Number: 2010900667

*Our mission is to efficiently provide the world's finest, most comprehensive book publishing
service, enabling every author to experience success. To find out how to publish your book, your
way, and have it available worldwide, visit us online at www.trafford.com*

Trafford rev. 1/5/10

North America & international
toll-free: 1 888 232 4444 (USA & Canada)
phone: 250 383 6864 ♦ fax: 812 355 4082

DEDICATION AND ACKNOWLEDGMENTS

Dedicated to three heroes of mine who exemplify that: "There is no way to peace, peace is the way!"

Bishop Carl Segerhammar– "Seger" who demonstrated the courage a leader needs for Peacemaking by his unwavering support despite pressure from a hostile University President and a misinformed public during my arrest and trial for my Active Nonviolent ministry.

Pastor Harold Sigmar– "Hal" who affirmed and accepted me, encouraging me to celebrate not only my accomplishments, but also my failures, as crucial steps in learning the ways of peace, demonstrating the qualities needed in any person of peace.

Pastor Robert Herhold– "Bob" whose deep spirituality was expressed in progressive political action, community involvement, published books, and everyday working for ways of peace, not the way of violence or war.

I heartily acknowledge that my wife Dru and companion on this journey for over 60 years, has been the peace-mate whose humor has kept me laughing, joy has kept me vital, and love has kept me strong, being the vital contributor to my Journey. I've exposed my three children to the extremities of the world, and their responses have blessed my life with their passions: Brad with his uncompromising opposition to uncivil corporate power, Kim with her advocacy for the immigrant and her deep spirituality, Scott with his gentleness for children and interpersonal relational skills.

I acknowledge the following groups and people as companions in this unfinished journey, without which I would not have kept my vision and commitment to peacemaking:

LUTHERAN PEACE FELLOWSHIP (LPF): national coordinator Glen Gersmehl, Leo Kohls, Jean Martensen, Barbara Rossing, Jon Nelson, Dan Erlander, Gary Kohls, Charles Lutz, John Schramn and many others.

FELLOWSHIP OF RECONCILIATION (FOR): Richard Deats, John Dear, Ernie Davis.

PACE e BENE: the Franciscan Nonviolence Center: Ken Butigan, Rosemary Lynch, Alain Richard, Julia Occhiogrosso.

CATHOLIC WORKER: Jeff Dietrich, Catherine Morris, John Dear, Ched Myers, Dan & Phil Berrigan, Jim Douglass.

INTERFAITH PEACE MINISTRY of Orange County (IPM): Dennis Short, Gwen Felton, Pat Hug, Don Will, Joyce Georgieff, Clif Churn, Lucille Sherman, Joan Lindroth, Kathy Schinhofen, George DeMitt, Muzammil Siddiqui, Suad Kesler, Bernie King.

CENTER ON CONSCIENCE AND WAR: Jean Martensen

WITNESS FOR PEACE: Joan Lindroth

CUERNAVACA CENTER FOR INTERCULTURAL DIALOGUE ON DEVELOPMENT (CCIDD): Ray Plankey, Bishop Sergio Méndez Arceo.

NONVIOLENT PEACEFORCE: Mel Duncun, David Hartsough.

NATIONAL FARM WORKER MINISTRY (NFWM): Chris Hartmier. Caesar Chavez, Virginia Nesmith, Jeanne & Roy Giordano.

LUTHERAN OFFICE OF PUBLIC POLICY (LOPP): Mark Carlson

SOJOURNERS: Jim Wallis, Duane Shank.

SIERRA CLUB: Vicky Hoover, John Muir.

EVERY CHURCH A PEACE CHURCH (ECAPC): Gary Kohls, John Stoner.

UNIVERSITY OF EAST AFRICA: Helen and David Kimble, Dennis Osborn, Bishop Moshi, Julius Nyerere, Nicolas Maro, Cuthbert Omari.

LONDON SCHOOL OF ECONOMICS AND POLITICAL SCIENCE (LSE): Richard Titmuss, David Kimble.

CAMPUS MINISTRY: Donald Heiges, Morris Wee, Henry Hetland, John Arthur, Don Hetzler, Evi Christenson, Father Peter Sammon, James Carr, Hal Sigmar, Verlyn Smith, Chuck Lewis, Herb Schmidt, Gus Shultz.

MOUNT OF OLIVES LUTHERAN CONGREGATION in Mission Viejo: In this conservative Orange County area there were so many people in this large congregation, in which I was Senior Pastor for 18 years, from whom I experienced love & friendship as well as being fellow peacemakers and workers for justice, colleagues ready to experiment with me in

Radical Discipleship and building 'Small Base Communities in an Affluent Society' paralleling the *communidades de base'* of Mexico and Latin America, that I won't begin to mention individuals, but am indebted to them for enriching my Unfinished Journey.

ST. JOHN'S LUTHERAN CONGREGATION in Sacramento: In this liberal California Capitol city, St. John's is a congregation of many progressive members involved in public life and justice causes.

THINKING ACTIVE SENIOR CLERGY (TASC): These retired clergy as a group have been a very supportive community in advocating for peace and justices causes.

I am grateful to the giants who have pioneered the Way of Active Nonviolence, especially Mahatma Gandhi who was inspired by the unconditional love ethic of Jesus and demonstrated its essentiality for social change, Martin Luther King, Jr. who built on both Jesus and Gandhi to demonstrate the Way of Nonviolent Direct Action for social change, and Caesar Chavez who built on both as he demonstrated that we were just beginning to understand the power of love and nonviolence, even as we were rapidly learning of the weakness of force and war.

Others who have contributed greatly to my Unfinished Journey are Walter Wink, Father Colman McCarthy, Bishop Stanley E. Olson, Gil Bailie, Teilhard de Chardin, Robert McAfee Brown, A. J. Muste, Daniel Berrigan, Dietrick Bonhoeffer, Gustavo Gutierrez, Paul Tillich, John Howard Yoder, James W. Douglass, Bishop Lowell O. Erdahl, Ronald J. Sider, Dom Helder Camara, Richard Deats, John Schramn, Thich Nhat Hanh, Thomas Merton, Paul Rogat Loeb, Jim Wallis, Arthur Waskow, Desmond Tutu, Nelson Mandela, Gary Kohls, Bill & Jean Lesher, John Paul Lederach, Rushworth M. Kidder, Marcus Borg, Rabbi Michael Lerner, and many others.

Contents

INTRODUCTION: SUMMER 2008: **When Did It All Change?** xiii

Part I: THE JOURNEY—BEGINNINGS 1

Chapter 1
AUGUST 6, 1945: **The Discovery of Fire** 3

Chapter 2
AUGUST 9, 1945: **Technological Giants and Moral Pygmies** 15

Chapter 3
SEPTEMBER 2, 1945: **Beginning All Over** 23

PART II: THE JOURNEY – THE STORM ALONG THE WAY 39

Chapter 4
1945—1960: **The Lull Before the Storm** 41

Chapter 5
1960s: **The Storm Builds—A Global View** 57

Chapter 6
1967-70: **The Storm Comes** 85

Chapter 7
1970—2000: **Dealing With the Storm's Aftermath** 107

PART III: THE JOURNEY—AN UNFINISHED JOURNEY 143

Chapter 8
JANUARY 1, 2000: **A New Beginning** 145

Chapter 9
SEPTEMBER 11, 2001: **An Awakening** 161

Chapter 10
SEPTEMBER 2, 2008: **Hope Renewed** 183

EPILOGUE   205

ABOUT THE AUTHOR   209

"Through the release of atomic energy, our generation has brought into the world the most revolutionary force since prehistoric man's discovery of fire. This basic force of the universe cannot be fitted into the outmoded concept of narrow nationalisms...We scientists recognize our inescapable responsibility to carry to our fellow citizens an understanding of atomic energy and its implication for society. In this lies our only security and our only hope—we believe that an informed citizenry will act for life and not for death.

—A. Einstein, 1947

INTRODUCTION

SUMMER 2008—When Did It All Change?

THE SUN HAD JUST risen over the Upper Yosemite Valley, breaking the early morning sleepy quiet atop the lookout from Glacier Point's fantastic view. I remembered the time nearly 70 years previous, when as a teenager I had first viewed the spectacular sight. But now my mind was swirling around trying to make sense of a host of competing memories

I remembered how life had appeared so simple 70 years ago. Seeming so peaceful and secure. And I remembered this spectacular sight from Glacier Point's 7000-foot elevation, looking down dizzily at the ant-like creatures walking in the Yosemite Valley 3000 feet below. And across the valley was Half Dome, towering 2000 feet higher than Glacier Point, tantalizingly daring me I thought, to try to conquer her majestic height. I remembered how the physical world of heights and depths had dwarfed and overwhelmed me even though my personal and social world felt safe, where all was peaceful and secure.

When did it all change? When did the idyllic life of comfort and confidence in the future that I had anticipated, change to the hectic ever changing, challenging, and often insecure and violent turmoil that had kept unfolding in my life. Earlier, I had believed, I lived in the greatest land in the world, America, a nation that everybody else in the world admired and looked up to. At least, I thought they did. God loved me—"Jesus loves me, this I know, for the Bible tells me so"—I had sung as a child. President Roosevelt had told us, my Dad said, that the depression was over. Dad's job had been getting better each year. High school graduation was just a few years away. What had promised to be a peaceful journey through life had become a journey full of violence, insecurity, and change?

When did it all change? Was it that day, August 6, 1945, out in the Pacific Ocean toward the end of World War II, while I was serving as a United States Marine aboard the USS Missouri battleship the day I heard the ship's loudspeaker saying "Now Hear This. We've just dropped a special bomb, an Atomic Bomb, on Hiroshima, destroying the city?" I remembered the cheers and bedlam of all the men: "Wonderful, it's over. Let's drop another on Tokyo and kill a million of the bastards" was the expressions of many of the excited sailors and marines. At first I was as excited as the others. Then I remembered going up on the bow of the ship, alone, surrounded by a mysterious presence and a host of questions, of disappointments, of hopes. What's happening to us... and to me...I wondered? A city destroyed, thousands of civilians, women and children, killed, and we... I... am cheering and wildly celebrating. Have we... have I... lost our humanity? Is this what happens to people in war? Is this really the way to peace? Is there a better way?

When did it all change? Was it that day a few days later on August 9th, when again we heard "Now Hear This! We have just dropped another Atomic Bomb on Nagasaki, destroying the entire city." I remembered wondering whether this was cause for celebration, or repentance? Wasn't this really an inexcusable atrocity? Were not we simply rationalizing our evil deeds, as our enemies rationalized the Holocaust or Pearl Harbor? Were we in danger of becoming simply a mirror image of the Nazis and the Japanese? Is this the way to peace, or is there a better way?

When did it all change? Was it that day September 2nd, 1945 aboard the battleship USS Missouri in Tokyo Bay, when the Peace Surrender was signed bringing World War II to an end? Although a mere teenage PFC Marine, I was honored to be part of the Honor Guard that day, standing near General Douglas MacArthur, Supreme Commander for the Allied Powers. My heart was thrilled as I heard General MacArthur say, "Today the guns are silent. A great tragedy has ended. A great victory has been won...the entire world lies quietly at peace. The holy mission has been completed." However, I was also seriously challenged when I heard MacArthur say, "We must go forward to preserve in peace what we won in war. We have had our last chance." There was no doubt in my mind: I must be a peacemaker, I resolved. My dream, my vision was to commit myself to helping make a world of true peace, of real justice, of realistic democracy, of loving community in the years ahead.

Or did it all change when I observed the short-sighted patriotism of so many of my war-mates. Or the anti-Semitism I so often observed. Or the self-righteousness and exaggerated claims of decency that I saw in so many of my fellow Americans, in spite of their prejudice toward the Japanese, and the looting and raping of Philippine villagers by some of my fellow marines. Or the racism that was part of military policy, or the racist behavior of so many of my shipmates? Or the abundance of blatant heterosexual disregard of moral values, even as they hypocritically condemned homosexuals, many of whom lived lives of high ethical commitment? Or was it later when... well, there had been so many other experiences in my life, I couldn't recount them all. Still I wondered when, and how, and why the world had so changed.

As I stood looking out over the valley below, recalling my lifelong journey, and the many surprises, the hurts and the joys, I wondered why had it all happened that way? Now, I wondered, what would the future be like? Were the tomorrows to be feared? Or dare I hope that, just as the rising sun was bringing warmth and brightness to life at Glacier Point and eventually the Yosemite Valley below, that new life and gladness and peace would also come to this world? Dare I hope, along with John Muir who loved Yosemite Valley and the inspiration of Glacier Point, that "This is still the morning of creation"? As exciting as the adventure had been in the past, I was sure of only one thing: It was an Unfinished Journey.

Part I:
THE JOURNEY—BEGINNINGS

"Ours is a world of nuclear giants and ethical infants. We know more about war than we know about peace, more about killing than we know about living."

—*General Omar Bradley*

Chapter 1

AUGUST 6, 1945: The Discovery of Fire

I WAS PROUD TO be a member of the United States Marine Corps. Only 10 days after graduating from High School as a 17-year old teenager, I proudly put on the uniform, ready to help make the world safe for democracy, or at least for America. Never had I considered being a soldier before December 7, 1941. However when a peace-loving nation like the USA could suffer an attack at Pearl Harbor, as FDR said on that 'Day of Infamy', it was time to step forward and defend ourselves, I thought. My Uncle Johnny suddenly became my hero. Uncle John, although a drop-out from high school earlier, and unable to get a job and almost forced by his parents to join the Marines to 'make a man out of yourself', suddenly became an example for me of what a 'real man' should be. Although still a private when the war started, Johnny soon became a corporal, and then 'gave his life' at Guadalcanal for freedom and for America. I could hardly wait to join up. And after seeing the beautiful Maureen O'Hara in the motion picture 'The Shores Of Tripoli', I lay awake nights imagining that all Marines had such romantic attractions, and could hardly wait to be so lucky.

But romance, and glory, wasn't coming to me that easily. In boot camp at San Diego, on the first day after being assigned my M1 rifle, I had made the mistake of referring to my rifle as a gun. Immediately I was forced to pay the penalty for the blunder of calling my rifle my gun, unimaginable for a marine. The penalty—embarrassingly was to stand bare naked in the 'head', with rifle in one hand and crotch in the other, shouting 50 times "This is my Rifle, this is my Gun; this is for Killing, this is for Fun!" I never made the mistake again. Then for the next six weeks, we were out of the barracks by 5:30 every morning. Immediately we were marched out to the boon-docks, and then made to crawl, often with our faces in the mud, on our bellies. Climbing walls and crawling over barriers on the obstacle course for an hour followed that. Just when we thought we were ready to go, we were put through a half hour of marching drills, before finally heading back to the barracks to clean up for chow. What really galled us as we headed back to our barracks was hearing 'reveille' being sounded at the navy base across the channel and knowing that the 'swabbies' were just getting out of the sack.

After the first week of boot camp, I was really looking forward to Sunday, when we were told we would be free for the day. Then when the first Sunday arrived, we were awakened from our sacks at 0530 with the usual "hit the deck – all out in formation in 10 minutes." One of our three Drill Instructors, Plt. Sgt. Franzi, ordered us to attention, then "right face, march" and we found ourselves headed out to the boon-docks just as we had the previous six days. The same routine was repeated of crawling, climbing, and marching until finally coming in for chow. After another horrible breakfast and back in our barracks, chief D.I. Plt. Sgt. Baleu, gave us the cheering news: "That's all the routine for the day, except we'll march you to meals. Now you're confined to the barracks for the day. Spit shine those field shoes till they shine, and be ready for inspection first thing in the morning. That's all."

"Dammit" the guy at the next cot mouthed silently, not daring for Sgt. Balen to hear him. "How we supposed to shine these shoes. We've marched through mud every day, waded through water, and marched in them till my dogs are barking complaints." All the other guys joined him with their bitching. It was at this point that 'Big Red' showed himself the real leader of the platoon. 'Big Red' was the Old Married Guy of the platoon, with a wife and child at home, at his old age of 25. He had been asked many times why he was in the Corps, but he never spoke a word all week. When the griping got pretty bad, he simply said: "What are you kids crying about? What did you think you were getting into? A boy's club?" And then he quietly showed how he had rubbed Kiwi into his boots until they almost looked like dress shoes. A little of the Marine Corps' favorite shoe polish, a little spit, and a lot of careful rubbing, and the rough leather of the boots began to take on a hard finish, until, like a mirror, you could see your face in the them. Soon the rest of us were competing to see who could get the best shine on their 'Boon Dockers!' Though few of us duplicated Big Red's efforts or got his results. Even then, we were all really disappointed when we discovered that the polish cracked and the shine disappeared after walking a short distance, and the effort had to be repeated all over again to get another good spit shine. We soon learned to spit shine our boots the last thing at night before inspections in the morning, if we didn't want to get into trouble when standing inspection. We also learned that walking carefully flat-footed helped keep the shine from cracking behind the toe of the boot. However, by 15 minutes following inspections the hard work to get a shine had to begin all over again. When we were finally given dress shoes after the 4th week, it seemed better than any Christmas present we had ever received.

While we were spit shining our boots that first Sunday morning, John, probably the youngest kid next to me in the platoon, came over to me and said "I thought we were supposed to get to go to chapel when we were in the military service?" I told him "Yeah, that's right, we do, don't we. Lets go up and ask for permission to go this morning." Together we walked up to the table at the front, where Sgt. Baleu was sitting, and stood at attention. "Requesting permission to go to chapel at 1000 this morning, sir." The Sgt. looked up, rather unbelievingly, and said, "What was that?" "Sir, we're requesting permission to go to chapel this morning, sir," I said. "Permission denied" he mumbled, and turned back his attention to the article he had been reading. John started to turn around and go back to his cot, when I blurted out "Sir, we understood that everyone in the service had the right to attend chapel while they were in the military." At this, the Sgt. looked up from his reading, and stared me in the eye for a long time. Finally he said, "Listen, in this Lash-Up, I'll be your almighty god and tell you everything you need to know. Understand?" At this, I nearly turned around to go, but after a moment said, "I understand, Sir. But we're requesting permission to go to chapel this morning, sir." At this, the Sgt. stood up, angry, red faced, and started to speak. Then he stopped, and simply stared at us. I stood there, wondering what was going to happen to me? Was it to be ordered to clean the heads for a week? Assigned to KP for the rest of boot camp? Maybe to be shot at sunrise?

After about a minute, which seemed an eternity to me, the Sgt. said "OK, fall out, out front at 0950 and I'll march you to chapel." Surprised, we turned around and went back to our cots. Shortly after, the Sgt. walked to the center of the barracks and announced "Anyone wishing to go to chapel this morning, fall out at 0950, out front, and I'll march you to chapel." That morning nearly every man in the platoon went to chapel, for many of them it was the first time in their lives that they had ever been in a church. And, in the following weeks they always had the opportunity to go to a chapel of their choice, although not many of them took advantage of it. To my surprise, though, Sgt. Balen continued going with us.

Later, back in the barracks, quite a discussion took place about what had happened that morning. A couple Catholics complained that it was a Protestant service they went to, and they were going to ask that in the future they get to go to a Catholic Mass. Several said it was a boring experience. John, who along with me was the one originally requesting to go, said it really didn't seem like church to him. Another said that he missed the music, while another said that in his church they taught that music was of the devil and wouldn't allow any. When one guy said he always had bread and wine at their church, another kid said he thought it wasn't proper to eat in church. I said I wondered what Jewish people or people of other religions did in the military, but one kid objected that this was a Christian country, and if others didn't like it they could leave. After this discussion, I had serious question about the religious or spiritual maturity of people, at least those I was meeting in the Marine Corps.

The next day, Sgt. Franzi told us he heard that a lot of us had gotten religion yesterday. He then taunted us: "That's good, because you're going to need it when you nearly get your ass shot off soon when you go overseas."

It was not long before we had finished our eight weeks of boot camp. Soon the platoon entered advanced training at Pendleton Marine base. But, on the second day of advanced training, we received the announcement that because of the high casualty rate of Marine wounded and dead in the capture of Japanese held islands in the Pacific, our advance training was being cut short, and we would be shipped overseas the following morning.

Before daybreak, we boarded the Victory Ship Pickaway, and were herded below deck in the bow of the ship. Not allowed to go topside till we were out of the harbor and at sea, I grabbed the second bunk up in the stack of five bunks, placed my pack along side my feet, and hung my helmet on the chain supporting the bunks After a couple hours out to sea, the vomit from seasick marines swished across the deck, from side to side, with a sickening smell that soon was worse than what our gunny sergeant called 'the smell of a Chinese whore house.' Sensing that I too was going to 'heave', I grabbed my helmet to puke in, only to learn that the fellow in the bunk above me had already used it to catch his puke. That was all that was needed for the fellow below me in his bunk to get sprayed with my contribution to the sickening vomit. At that point, despite the command to stay below decks, I and others said "to hell with it" and went up topside for air, where we remained for all eight days in our passage to Pearl Harbor. Twice a day we went down one deck to the mess hall, where the temperature was about 110 degrees, for grub that was more fit for cattle than humans. The glory of the Corps was getting dimmer and dimmer, and the romance was totally missing. After eight days of this glorious cruise, we arrived in Pearl Harbor. After a few days taking on supplies in Pearl, we headed out again for thirteen days en route to Guam, thankful that neither Japanese subs nor planes were encountered. I began wondering, "where is the glory, where is the romance, and where are the girls that I had dreamed of?"

I soon discovered that neither glory nor romance was to be found on the island of wartime Guam. Never had I seen so much red mud, mosquitoes, spam, rain and fighting in my whole life. When it wasn't the enemy we were fighting, we fought among ourselves. It was as if, since we had joined the Marines to fight, and the enemy wasn't handy just then, we had to look to our own for a good fight. All of us had a few marine officers that we would really like to take down, though that would have landed us in the brig. And, anyway, there were no officers around. The officers were all quartered in permanent-type buildings, ate at the officer's mess, and were enjoying the glory and romance they had dreamed about. As for the army, we hadn't seen hide or hair of any of them in the Pacific area. As for the navy, those guys had their dry sacks to sleep in, good hot food three times a day, and safety aboard their relatively luxurious ships out there. So, naturally, the fights were with the only people available, the other marines in our own outfit, even good buddies. 'Big Red', 'the Old Married Guy' with a wife and child at home, at his old age of 25 years, seemed the only peacemaker in our group. Big Red told us that he had seen enough fighting at home, and joined the marines to get a little peace, so he was constantly yelling at us to "just knock it off and quit all this fighting". We thought he was a weirdo.

After one of the typically rainy, sweaty, muddy, hectic, futile days, Donald, one of my pals, came up with an offer I couldn't refuse. My pal Donald had been an all American football player in his freshman year before enlisting, and had been offered what he thought was a fantastic opportunity. It seems the Corps was determined to find a way to get him to play on one of their football teams, in competition with other military teams. Although playing on a team would have to wait until later, the Corps was anxious to find him the best place to serve until he could actually compete on one of their teams. A navy ship was in the harbor, needing several marines to join its detachment aboard ship. Donald was offered the chance to be one of them, and they gave him permission to ask one of his buddies to also be assigned to the ship. It seems "brown nosing" was a common practice even in the Corps. Donald didn't know anything about the ship, but the idea of a dry sack to sleep in, no mud to tramp in, no mosquitoes to fight, and three square meals a day sounded too good to miss. I quickly said, "take me." Later, when I thought about it, I realized that this was not something I had been 'ordered' to do, rather it was the first real 'choice' opportunity I had since I had chosen to join the marines.

I had absorbed the Marine Corps' tradition of hating anything Navy—its ships, its enlisted men that we called 'swabbies', and its officers, which we called 'glorified ushers'. But even I had to admit that when I first saw the ship we had been assigned to, I was both surprised and thrilled. It was Battleship 63, none other than the USS Missouri. Over three football-fields long, with 3000 men on board (the Marines would say over 2900 Swabbies, and about 40 men— Marines) it was probably the newest and grandest ship afloat. It was the third ship in the history of the U.S. Navy to bear the name Missouri.

Admiring the big Battleship Missouri came easy, although learning the Navy language took a while longer. Almost the first thing I said upon seeing the 'Big Mo' was "Wow, what a boat!" when the 'swabbie' taking us aboard immediately bawled me out. "Listen buddy —Never call this a 'boat'. Boats are things like tugboats or rowboats. This is a ship—and dammit, the biggest and best ship the Navy has ever seen. Call this a boat again and you're gonna end up in the brig." I was soon to learn words like 'bulkheads, 'fore and aft,' and 'port and starboard,' as part of the new language.

We were to learn that the first ship to bear the name Missouri was launched in 1841, mounted with two 10 inch and eight 8 inch guns. (I still was a little nervous calling anything a 'gun', after my embarrassing experience in boot camp.) The second was launched in 1901, mounted with ten 12-inch guns and sixteen 6-inch guns. It was one of the ships chosen to make a world cruise in 1908, visiting Japan to try to cement friendship between the two nations. (I often wondered how appropriate battleships were to indicate friendship?) This second Missouri finally became one of the ships sacrificed and scrapped in 1924, as part of the agreements made in 1919 at the end of WWI at the Washington Conference on Limitation of Naval Armaments. It seems that even back then people had been determined to end all wars.

That determination and hope had obviously been given up when in 1939 the construction of the third U.S.S. Missouri was authorized by act of Congress. I was still in High School when the keel was laid on Jan. 6, 1941 and some of the hull and fire rooms had already been built when the Japanese (they were called Japs back then, and depicted as wild-eyed fanatics hardly human) struck Pearl Harbor on Dec. 7, 1941. Work on the ship ceased, and was not resumed until Jan. 25, 1943, when 5000 men resumed work on her daily in Brooklyn Navy Yard. This, the third ship of the U.S. Navy to be named Missouri, the present one, was launched Jan. 19, 1944. Former senator Harry Truman, then vice president, gave the speech. He would in the following year become president. Finally, it was commissioned June 11, 1944, and immediately sent to the Pacific as part of the US fleet fighting the war.

It was February of the following year before the Missouri was involved in its first fighting action. As part of Task force 58, off the island of Iwo Jima, they shot down their first Japanese airplane; the first of five or six they would be credited with having shot down. Another time they encountered Japanese Kamikaze planes, downing one into the sea just short of the ship. A second Kamikaze came in with a murderous hail of fire, crashing into the starboard quarter on the main deck level before finally crashing into the 5-inch mount and exploding in fire. Fortunately little serious damage was done. The pilot's mutilated body parts had been scattered onto the main deck, and together with parts of the plane, quickly thrown over the side into the sea.

Even in the midst of war there are lulls that are like a breath of fresh air in one's life. Such was the several days of lay over that the Missouri had in the southern Philippine Islands. Laying offshore in the Leyte Gulf, each day for three days different parts of the crew and detachment went ashore for 'R&R,' rest and recreation. The only thing there was beach, the sea, and an allotment of two bottles of beer for each fellow. Someone must have lost count, because most everyone had a half dozen of the cans of beer without labels, which made for some wild football games, sand fights, and regular fights. Outnumbered fifty-to-one, we marines more than held our own.

It was rumored that there was a small village a mile inland, and some guys took the challenge to explore the rumor. I was curious about the local customs and wanted to explore the village, and was invited to join those going, but decided not to go. Several hours later, a half dozen fellows returned, boasting that they not only partook of the native local cooking, but also of the rape of the native young girls in the village. "That's what the Nips did in China to the Chinese women" they said "and we just returned the favor." When confronted with the fact that the locals were not the enemy, and were our allies, they simply answered, "what's the difference—a f--- is a f---."

Back on ship, three of us reflected on the day's happenings. We agreed that one of the realities of war is that no matter the virtue of original intentions in going to war, both sides soon begin to adopt the tactics of the other side, and the original purpose seems to get lost in the process. Also, I wondered what I would have done had I gone with the others into the village. Was I also losing sight of why I chose to become a marine in the first place?

While the fighting on Okinawa was going on, the Missouri was called to bombard the enemy positions confronting our Marines on the island. With only a few hundred yards separating the two positions, this was almost impossible to do safely without hitting our own troops as well, despite the sophisticated technology we possessed. Our ship did the bombarding from many miles offshore on open seas, with shells from our 16-inch guns. Supposedly, airplane spotters would give corrections for miscalculations in our gunnery, but prayers were being offered that our shells would do more damage to the enemy than to our own troops.

It was months later that I learned that 'Big Red', the Old Married Man of our platoon in boot camp, had been killed by shells from our own ships at sea, which were supposedly being lobbed over their heads onto the enemy. When my buddies from my former platoon learned that the Missouri was one of those ships, and that when I had left them on Guam it was to go aboard the Missouri, they were almost ready to kill me. I also wondered, would I have been killed by 'friendly fire' had I stayed behind with them?

By July of 1945, American strikes against Japanese cities were encountering little resistance. The Missouri and other ships bombarded the northern city of Muroran on the island of Hokkaido of Japan, the second bombardment the Japs had felt on their sacred home islands in as many days. Two days later we struck industrial targets in Hitachi, only sixty miles from Tokyo. It was obvious that Japanese resistance was nearly nonexistent, and that an invasion of Japan would soon begin. Many of the navy's personnel on the ship were training for landing operations. Although the marine detachment was assigned to serve aboard ship, we were informed that we should expect to take part in landing operations, which duplicated the original purposes of the U.S. Marines 'From the Halls of Montezuma to the Shores of Tripoli.' To prepare for this invasion special physical exercises were the order of the day, and assault-landing tactics were carefully being rehearsed. We were expecting to invade any day.

August 6 dawned as just another day. I cleaned and oiled the 20mm antiaircraft gun I was assigned to, and was doing some physical exercises toughening up for a possible assault landing, when a special announcement came over the ship loudspeaker. "Now hear this! Now hear this! We have received a report that American bombers have dropped a special kind of bomb, called an 'atomic bomb', on the Japanese city of Hiroshima, totally destroying the city of two-hundred-thousand people. That is all we know at the moment." Stunned for the moment, cheers and bedlam soon broke out aboard ship. "Wonderful," "fantastic," and "lets drop it on Tokyo and kill a million of the bastards" were the expressions of many excited swabbies and marines. Chaos reigned supreme among the celebrating crew. "We won" and "It's nearly over" were the popular expressions. I was as excited as everyone else.

Then as confirmation of the total destruction of a major Japanese city was confirmed, I began to have second thoughts. That night, wanting to be alone with my thoughts, I went forward to the bow of the ship.

It was quiet, with only the sea smacking the ship as it plowed through the water. It was dark, only the stars shining in the sky. I was alone, yet surrounded by a mysterious presence and a host of questions, of disappointments, of hopes. Atomic Bombs? Destruction of entire cities in mere moments? I felt the same way that the early cave men must have felt when they discovered fire! I was overwhelmed with awe. Or was it fear? Or hope? This changes everything. I felt the possibilities— for good—and for evil.

What's happening to us, I wondered? What's happening to me? A city destroyed, thousands of civilians, women and children, killed, and we... I... am cheering and wildly celebrating. What about the value of life, the sacredness of life, whether they be friend or foe? Have we lost our humanity? Is this what happens to people in war? I found myself sobbing, unable to stop shedding tears. And then other thoughts came to the surface: Is this really the way to peace? Is there a better way? Does war reduce every one to the sub-human level? And a very personal question confronted me: What do I want to do with the rest of my life?

"We still have a choice today: nonviolent co-existence or violent co-annihilation: Nonviolence or Nonexistence."

—*Martin Luther King, Jr.*

Chapter 2

AUGUST 9, 1945: Technological Giants and Moral Pygmies

IF WE THOUGHT THE announcement on August 6, 1945 meant peace had returned, we were badly mistaken. The first thing we heard when the detachment was called to formation was Sgt. Gaby proclaiming "get your weak minds out of the clouds and your asses off the deck and get ready for the real thing." It was clear as far as he was concerned that the 'real thing' was getting ready for the invasion of Japan. Physical and tactical training was doubled, and the expectation grew that we would soon be going ashore in the attack on the Japanese mainland. Second Lt. Kellin expanded his patriotic lectures on the glory of Marine Corps history, recounting the honors that leathernecks had earned from Tripoli up through Guadalcanal and Iwo Jima until today. Now, he said, it would be our opportunity to add our part soon as we got the chance to really prove our patriotism. Some of our guys could hardly keep from laughing, since Kellin himself was one of those 21-year old '90 day wonders' with a bit of college and officers' training at Camp Lejune prior to coming aboard a few weeks back. We knew however it wouldn't be a laughing matter if he were the one leading us into combat.

These were difficult days for me. It was not the additional tough training, but rather, dealing in my own mind with Hiroshima and the dropping of that special bomb. I had no idea what an atomic bomb was, although I knew it was many times more powerful than anything else previously available in wartime. I remembered, that while still a civilian in high school, I had thought the Nazis were barbarian when they dropped bombs on London's civilian population, killing hundreds of defenseless people. However, after our side had gained military advantage, we outdid them in our destruction of German cities. Initially, I had applauded these efforts. Now I wondered whether we had become just as barbarian in our efforts?

Len, one of the marines that often joined Rosen and me in discussing subjects other than women and sports surprised us both when he said, "you guys are so naïve." Len, a Mormon from Utah, was one of the older guys in the detachment, had four years of college before joining the Marine Corps and was usually pretty quiet. "Why get so excited about this Atomic Bomb thing" he said, "it's no worse than what we have been doing all along." He reminded us that our own 16-inch shells from miles off shore probably killed many more civilians than military personnel. Even worse, we had been systematically dropping conventional bombs, as well as the even more destructive firebombs, on most of the major Japanese cities for months, probably killing a million or more civilians, including women and children, as we were destroying their cities.

It really surprised me when Len said he wanted to be a pacifist. He acknowledged that he really wasn't a practicing pacifist, because he fell far short of actually living like a pacifist. This was the first time I had ever met a pacifist, or at least a person who wanted to be one, and I wanted to know more. Len said pacifism was not part of the Mormon tradition, and he had received no support from them. Because he needed the support of his church to qualify as a conscientious objector, and he lacked that support, he knew that when he finished college, he would have been drafted. To beat the draft, he volunteered to join the marines. He reasoned that he could do this in good conscience, because he believed even pacifists could fight to defend their country when it was threatened. However, he felt that, even when defending his family from attack or defending one's country from attack, indiscriminate killing of defenseless people was wrong, not only for our enemies, but also especially for us. When pressed further, Len said that he felt the heart of pacifism was not so much how one reacted to attack, but what one did long before any attack took place. It was during normal times that we should act to prevent the development of conditions that caused people to be poor, or to feel dominated, or to get angry. The real issue, he thought, was not war, rather what was done to prevent them. Once war began, barbaric behavior usually became rationalized as not only acceptable, but ethical and patriotic as well.

This was the first time I had seriously encountered the idea of pacifism, and for me it was a revolutionary idea. I didn't know much about Mormons, even though I had been taught that 'Mormons' were wrong. Len too believed that his church was wrong about pacifism. Though otherwise he said he was a practicing Mormon, and it seemed to me that he expressed and lived by ethical ideas that had eluded me in my own Christian Protestant experience. I wondered what my own church taught about pacifism? Why hadn't I learned of it during my growing up? Would they have supported me had I refused to join the military? And maybe most of all I wondered what Jesus would have said and done about war and killing and doing what I was doing?

It was during these days that our 3-way discussion grew into nightly conversations. Usually we talked on deck in the darkness of the night under the stars, often up on the bow of the ship where no one would bother us. If the seas were too rough, we could usually find a quiet spot someplace on the fantail of the ship.

It was on one of these nights that Rosen talked of his experience. He wasn't a pacifist, he said, because growing up a Jew in Brooklyn had required him to be ready every day to defend himself from those who hated "us Jew bastards". I began to realize how isolated and protected I had been growing up. As far as I could remember, Rosen was the first Jew I had ever really known and been close to. Rosen said that he was not a "religious Jew", whatever that meant. He said that being a Jew had not meant much to him until a few years earlier, when his family talked about the Holocaust. When they talked about several million Jews being killed deliberately in Germany and Poland under the Nazis, he decided that he would join the fighting in this war. Rosen claimed that Roosevelt had ignored the plight of the Jews in Europe, and suggested that even the Pope had supported Hitler in dealing with the Jews. He said he had heard that the Danes and Norwegians had been among the few to heroically act to save Jews, but that most Europeans and the rest of the world really shared in the suffering inflicted on the Jews. When I said I would have thought that Christians, at least, would have sprung to their defense, Rosen really became agitated. "The damned Christians are the worst. Ever since Martin Luther had called the Jews 'Christ Killers' hundreds of years ago, Luther's followers had been persecutors of Jews, and laid the foundation for Hitler's hatred and plans for eliminating them from the face of the earth."

I had a hard time accepting Rosen's comments. It took time, before I increasingly came to realize that what he said was true. To tell the truth, I became convinced only after an experience one evening as the three of us sat talking. One of the men came by who had been part of the group that had gone into the nearby village when they were on the beach on the Gulf of Leyte. Noticing Rosen, he said to me, "keep associating with that 'Jewboy' and you'll be in trouble too." Later, Rosen said that was the kind of comment he heard all the time, even here aboard ship.

I began to wonder about this discrimination. Why hadn't I heard before of the enormity of the holocaust? Was my family, my church, my friends part of a conspiracy against Jews, if not actively, at least silently? Did my nation and its leaders share in the persecution of Jews, either actively or silently? And how could Christians, when Jesus himself was a Jew, stand by and share in the persecution of the Jews, either actively or silently? I wondered!

The more they talked, the more disturbed I became. Then one evening after Rosen had told of his Jewish experience, Len felt free enough to tell us more about himself. It seems his pacifist leanings weren't the primary reason he had not been received well in his own community at home. Len said that even in his young teen years he never sensed the same attraction toward girls that most of his friends were experiencing and talking about. By the time he was in college, he had to admit to himself that he had no heterosexual attraction. Although he had never entered into a homosexual relationship, when he acknowledged to a counselor his feelings, he was quickly labeled a homosexual. When his family was informed of this, they demanded that he begin dating girls, and when he refused, he was ostracized from their home and family and church. Celibacy was not a problem for him, he said, and he had even briefly explored Catholicism because of this, but soon gave that up. It was not the faith that was his problem, but their refusal to accept who he felt he was, even though he had never engaged in any sexual conduct.

Len told me and Rosen that this was only the second time he had acknowledged this to anybody, and only because he trusted us and hoped to find acceptance from someone. The only other time he had shared this information with anyone since he had left home was shortly after beginning advanced training after boot camp. Two of his best friends in boot camp and in advanced training were sharing experiences, and he felt confident enough to share what he had just shared with us. Their response was to tell him he was a fag, and actually had beaten up on him when they were outside camp on their next liberty.

It seemed to me that the world was changing around me faster than I could deal with it. I really had no strong feelings about sexual orientations, and had never dealt face to face with someone who called himself a homosexual. I knew that I deeply respected Len, generally shared his outlook on other issues in life, and knew that Len was a most moral and ethical person. Why were labels so important? After observing so much unethical and irresponsible heterosexual activity the last few years, how could anyone condemn a person whose ethical and responsible actions was beyond reproach, simply because he was homosexual?Why were people so threatened by those who were simply different?

The morning of the 9th of August seemed to be just another day as we continued our special preparations for the invasion, although many thought the war was approaching its end. It had been reported that Japan's Foreign Minister Togo had said as early as July 13th, 1945: "Unconditional surrender is the only obstacle to peace." In other words, simply conceding a post-war figurehead position for the Japanese emperor might bring the war to a close. Then later that day, August 9th, another announcement came over the loudspeaker system: "Now hear this! Now hear this! We have just received word that another special bomb, an 'atomic bomb', has been dropped on the city of Nagasaki, destroying the entire city. We will keep you informed as further information comes in!" Although the shouting and celebration was tremendous, it seemed more restrained than the announcement that had been made after the Hiroshima bombing a few days earlier.

Sgt. Gabby argued that this bomb was dropped for the same reason the first bomb was dropped. He said it was "to send a message to those communist bastards, the Russians, that we have this bomb that can destroy any enemy." He argued that although out of necessity America had accepted the communists as allies during this war, America knew all along that communism would be as great a threat to America as were the Nazis. He said it was anticipated that the Russians would finally enter the war against Japan, and indeed the Soviet Union did declare war on Japan on August 8th. However, most of the men were arguing that we really dropped this second bomb to convince the Japanese that we would destroy them unless they surrendered first. And 'destroy them' is really what many of our men wanted to do.

I went to bed that night more confused than ever. Does it mean the war is nearly over? If so, that would be a good thing, and if destroying cities and people was necessary to end it, then that too might be a necessary and good thing. But was it? Wasn't dropping such terribly destructive bombs, and killing hundreds of thousands of people, really inexcusable atrocities? Were we simply just rationalizing our evil deeds, as our enemies rationalized the Holocaust or Pearl Harbor? If the victors really get to write the histories of wars, and if our enemies had won this war, would we have been tried as war criminals? Were we simply the mirror image of the Nazis and the Japanese? As General Omar Bradley was later to say, "We have become a nation of Technological Giants and Moral Pygmies." I began asking myself the question, does anyone really win a war, or does everybody lose?

"A great tragedy has ended. A great victory has been won. We must go forward to preserve in peace what we won in war. A new era is upon us. We have had our last chance. If we will not devise some greater and more equitable system, Armageddon will be at our door."

— General Douglas McArthur

HIROSHIMA (AUGUST 6, 1945)
(COURTESY OF U.S. DEPT. OF ENERGY)

GENERAL MACARTHUR SIGNS PEACE SURRENDER OF JAPAN
ABOARD U.S.S. MISSOURI, SEPTEMBER 2, 1945 IN TOKYO BAY
(COURTESY OF U.S. NAVY)

JERRY ABOARD U.S.S. MISSOURI

HONOR GUARD AT SURRENDER (SEPTEMBER 2, 1945)
JERRY- 3rd MAN, FRONT ROW
(COURTESY OF U.S. MARINE CORPS)

CERTIFICATE OF PRESENCE AT
PEACE SURRENDER

JERRY'S DOG TAG (3 YEARS WEAR)

JERRY AND HIS THREE BROTHERS-IN-LAW (ALL IN SERVICE)

22

Chapter 3

SEPTEMBER 2, 1945: Beginning All Over

OUR MARINE DETACHMENT'S ENTIRE routine changed shortly after the August 9th bombing of Nagasaki. Special training for the invasion seemed to stop, and I had increased time for my visits to the ship's library. Since coming aboard ship, the library had become my chief outlet for boredom, while providing stimulation for creative thought. Located down two decks on the aft of the ship, it became for me a safe place of retreat from always being surrounded by people. Although the Missouri was a very large ship, being surrounded by three thousand men in such close quarters proved especially confining. The quiet of the library not only provided a place of privacy and relaxation, but the books offered a fresh world of discovery. Earlier, I began keeping a journal of my readings aboard ship, and was surprised when I had listed over 100 books that I had read or perused carefully. For me, the library aboard ship introduced and encouraged my journey of discovery about other parts of the world, of areas of knowledge that I had never encountered before, and of history and authors and spiritual frontiers beyond my previous awareness.

It was in the library one evening that I began one of my more interesting relationships while aboard ship. While reading in the library that evening, one of the Negro sailors came in and started reading. Most of the workers in the Mess Hall were Negroes, and I had not gotten to know any of them. Wanting to be friendly, I asked what his name was. "I'm George," he said, and before anything else could be said, another sailor entered the library room. The new guy gave me an odd stare, and said, "I didn't think they were allowed in here!" and walked out. "What was that all about?" I asked George. "Some of the crew don't believe we Negroes should be allowed in the library, though I've been coming in here in the evenings when I get the chance, and I refuse to let them keep me out." Over the next few evenings I learned that his full name was "George Washington." Later, George explained there was another "George Washington" as well as a "George Washington Carver" in their mess hall group. He told me the names had been selected by parents in honor of either the first president or the educator/scientist named Carver. However, he told me, he personally didn't think it was an honor to be named after either of them, the president being a racist and the Negro educator being a "kiss-ass-brown-noser."

After this conversation, it was midnight and both of us were due for our watch. Since our compartments were on the first lower deck near each other, I suggested we walk forward together. George said that wouldn't be wise, that I might get myself in trouble with my fellow marines. Even worse, he said, he might get himself in danger of being beaten up by marines if we were seen together, unless it was an emergency or in an attack situation. I said that was ridiculous, but George was adamant, and insisted that I "wake up to reality."

Later, I told my buddies Len and Rosen about this conversation, and both agreed with what George said. Apparently, months earlier, before I was assigned to the Missouri, several Marines had beaten up on one of the Negro stewards who had wandered through the Marine quarters. Even though the Negroes were quartered immediately forward of the Marine detachment's quarters, which partly surrounded the #2 sixteen inch turret, Negroes had been warned that they were not to pass through the Marine quarters, even though it was their shortest route to the Mess Hall. Both 'Big Jim' and 'Rusty' of our marine detachment were from the South, and took it upon themselves to enforce the segregation practices that they had been raised under before entering the Corps. "They know better than infringing on white people's lives, and giving one of those 'niggers' the right to enter our space would begin the destruction of our Southern Way of Life," they drawled. And so, in the dark of an evening, they had taught the Negro steward a lesson, one holding while the other showered blows upon him, sending him to sick bay with multiple injuries. When I asked what had happened to Big Jim and Rusty following this, they answered "apparently nothing." After all, the Navy felt that it had moved race relations forward by simply allowing Negroes to serve in the Navy, even though they were not allowed to serve in any capacity other than as mess hall attendants

In later conversations I learned that George claimed to be a strong supporter of President Roosevelt. However, he insisted that even Roosevelt wouldn't offend the white southern politicians in the south by pushing for a bill against lynching, still a common practice that held his people down. George seemed well informed about politics in America or at least in the South where he lived. He argued that segregation of Negroes from whites in the armed forces was firmly enforced. Although Roosevelt had signed an executive order establishing the Fair Employment Committee, George claimed that Roosevelt had only signed because Philip Randolph, head of the Sleeping-Car Porters Union, had threatened a massive protest in the Capitol in 1941. However, George claimed, the order was seldom enforced, and nothing had really changed. Then he quoted from memory a poem Langston Hughes had written:

"What happens to a dream deferred?
Does it dry up like a raisin in the sun?
Or fester like a sore—And then run?
Does it stink like rotten meat?
Or crust and sugar over—like a syrupy sweet?
Maybe it just sags like a heavy load.
Or does it explode?"

George revealed a hidden anger that I had not seen before. "It's going to explode some day, you can count on it!" Then he said a strange thing: "Meet me up on the bow tonight at 10, I have a friend I want you to meet."

That night George introduced me to Reggie, whom I had never met. Reggie had a seriousness about him that I had never experienced before. Reggie quickly said: "I usually don't talk to you mother-fuckin'-whites, cuz most of you are worse than the Klan, talkin' big-talk but never doin nothin bout it. But George swears you're OK, so I agreed to come up. Why we niggers are out here, I don't even know. This damn war doesn't mean a thing to me. This damn Navy only lets us serve as messmen because they couldn't find anything lower. Jim crow is as bad in the military as it is in Alabama. Lynching continues, and it's not just the Klan, but also all you fuckin-white-bastards. The Red Cross won't even take our blood, fraid it will get into your lily-white veins. Fighting for what? Why should we even be here? This damned war doesn't mean a thing to me. Even if we win, we lose. When we go home, we still won't be hired, won't be allowed in the labor union, to live the life of 'colored only'. What we fighting for? Hitler couldn't do nothin worse to us than America does. These Japs are closer kin to us than you guys are. It's not the Germans and Japs that we hate—it's America!"

With that, he turned around and left. George then quietly told me "Reggie speaks for me too! And he speaks for most of the others also. Now, I better get below too, before others see us and I get into trouble."

I grew increasing perplexed by this encounter with the race issue. It had seemed to me that the Negroes I had known in my life always seemed happy. I would never call them 'nigger', although I remembered that my uncle had called them that and no one objected. I also remembered that even my dear Aunt Tanta one day as we had been out driving in the neighborhood had said "it looks like it might rain— see that black cloud over there!" And when I looked, all I saw was a black man walking down the street. I wondered whether my kindly dear Aunt Tanta was prejudiced? Surely not! I could believe it about my Uncle John however. But what about me, I wondered? Then I thought about Levi, a Negro friend of mine in High School, one of the most-liked kids in school, who had been president of the senior class, and had always said "Yes, sir" and "Yes, ma'am" when talking to any of the teachers. I wondered whether Levi might have had some of this same anger inside. Had Levi simply been doing what he had to do in order to be accepted?

And then I remembered Tac, one of the Takahashi family, a Japanese friend of mine in high school. Both Tac and his brother had been stars on the football team, and were popular throughout the school. Then one day Tac was suddenly missing from school, and after a few days we learned that Tac and his family had been evacuated from the coast to a detention camp up in the desert. Supposedly, people feared they might be dangerous aliens, with loyalty to Japan rather than America. But Tac was a third generation citizen, as much American as any of us. Was this part of the 'Red Peril' that we had studied in history class? And then I remembered that at the time neither I or my family or our close friends had protested against this evacuation.

Maybe even the liberal society that I had grown up in, including my friends, my family, and myself, were part of a racist society that looked good on the outside, but inside was really just as racist as Big Jim and the redneck South? I wondered about this that night as I fell asleep.

While I was having these meaningful personal experiences, life on board the Missouri was rapidly moving toward a worldwide important happening. Now I realized that it had seemed to be moving that way ever since May 18th, 1945, when the USS Missouri became the fighting flagship of Admiral William F. Halsey, USN, and Commander of the Third Fleet. With his four star flag flying from the Missouri, Admiral Halsey had led the final and climactic strokes of the war against Japan. For three and half years he had fought and led practically all the major sea battles of the pacific war. Now, as Admiral Halsey had come aboard the Missouri as flagship of the Third Fleet, he was to lead us to the final victory.

Increasingly the scuttlebutt and rumor was that the Japanese wanted to end the war. Finally, on August 15th we heard the loudspeakers proclaim: "Now hear this! Now hear this!! JAPAN SUES FOR PEACE, AND SURRENDERS." Again, cheers filled the air; the men hugged one another, and told one another "Now we can go home". However even this celebration was somewhat subdued, much quieter, and less passionate than the demonstration that had taken place after the announcement about the Atomic Bomb being dropped on Hiroshima August 6th, or even later after Nagasaki on August 9th. It seemed that Victory produced a lesser emotional charge than Revenge had produced following the A-Bomb attack. The popular feeling seemed to be that the Japanese were getting off easy, and that they deserved more punishment.

In the 'Missouri News Flash' printed later that day and given to us, it said:

"EXTRA—JAPAN SURRENDERS. At sea, off Tokyo, 15 August 1945. On August 14th, President Truman announced to the people of the world that Japan had surrendered unconditionally. The announcement was made simultaneously in Washington, Moscow, London and Chungking. The text of the President's statement is as follows. 'I have received this afternoon a message from the Japanese Government in reply to the message forwarded to that Government by the Secretary of State on August 11, 1945. I deem this reply an acceptance of the Potsdam Declaration, which specified the Unconditional Surrender of Japan. Arrangements are now being made for the formal signing of the Treaty at the earliest possible moment. General Douglas MacArthur has been appointed the Supreme Allied Commander to receive the Japanese surrender. Great Britain, Russia and China will be represented by high-ranking officers. Meanwhile the Allied Armed Forces have been ordered to suspend all offensive action. The Proclamation of VJ-Day must wait upon the formal signing of the surrender terms by Japan.'"

On the second page was the following:

"MESSAGE OF ADMIRAL WILLIAM F. HALSEY COMMANDER THIRD FLEET TO THE OFFICERS AND MEN OF THE THIRD FLEET 15 AUGUST 1945: The war is ended. You in conjunction with your brothers in arms of all services have contributed inestimably to this final result. Our fighting men have brought an implacable treacherous and barbaric foe to his knees in abject surrender. This is the first time in recorded history of the misbegotten Japanese race that they as a nation have been forced to submit to this humiliation. The forces of righteousness and decency have triumphed. Victory is not the end. Rather it is but the beginning. We must establish a peace, a firm, a just, and an enduring peace; a peace that will enable all decent nations to live without fear and in prosperity. Never again should we permit the enslavement of decent human beings—never again should tyrants be permitted to rise in a civilized world. The enemy over the entire world is conquered and has been forced to bow his collective knee to us the victors. We must in conjunction with all Allied forces so employed reduce Nippon to military impotency. We must keep them militarily impotent. It is imperative that instrumentalities be set up to educate and divorce the Japanese from their barbaric traditions, teachings and thoughts. To all of you belongs the credit. And I shall do all within my limited powers to see that you receive it."

I wrote home the next day: "Dear Mom and Dad. It's hard to believe, isn't it? A few days ago we were at war. Now it's over, only the occupation remains. On the day we received the news (August 15 out here) air strikes from our Task Force 38 were on the way to the Tokyo area. Word was flashed to them to return. We were instructed to break out our battle flags and blow our whistles and sirens in honor of this great occasion. However, we had to continue on alert status because, although the war was over, we weren't sure that all Japanese forces knew this. In the forward areas it takes time to notify all the forces and order them to stop fighting. For the last weeks, our task force has made air strikes on the Tokyo area, and bombarded the Japanese coast with our 16-inch guns from 15 miles away. This is the first time I have been able to write things like this, since our mail will no longer be censored under wartime conditions.

I guess I am proud to have helped win the war, and hope this is the last time that a war has to be won. One of my buddies insists no one can win a war any more than one can win an earthquake. He thinks we have become as barbaric in the process of carrying on this war as our enemies have been. After reading Halsey calling the Japanese "treacherous and barbaric" and referring to ourselves as "the forces of righteousness and decency", and remembering some of the things we Americans have done, maybe my buddy is right? Another buddy, who tries to be a pacifist, says the only way to win a war or to overcome an enemy is to make them your friend, and he quotes Jesus who said such things as "overcome evil with good" and "love your enemies". I don't know. Sometimes I think they are right. Anyway, I hope to see you soon. Love, Jerry."

During these anxious days of waiting for the formal end of the war, I was fortunate in getting to know Leroy, one of the Navy personnel assisting a Catholic chaplain. According to Leroy, the chaplain knew a good deal about the Japanese, and especially the history of Christianity in Japan. Leroy told me that the chaplain had told him his heart was really heavy hearing the announcement about the bombing of Nagasaki on August 9th. He had heard from reports that the city was destroyed with probably no survivors. From his studies, he knew that Nagasaki was famous in the history of Japanese Christianity as being the site of the largest Christian church in the Orient, St. Mary's Cathedral, and the largest concentration of Christians in all of Japan. Francis Xavier, the legendary Jesuit missionary, had established the mission church there in 1549. The Christian community thrived there until early in the 1600s when it became the target of brutal Japanese Imperial persecutions. And so a half-century after Xavier's mission was planted, it had become a capital crime simply to be a Christian. Then a reign of terror similar to the Roman persecutions in the early centuries decimated the Christian population of Nagasaki. It had been commonly believed that Christianity had been stamped out in Japan. However 250 years later, after the American Commodore Perry's gunboat diplomacy had opened up Japan to American trade, it was discovered that there were still thousands of baptized Christians living there in a catacomb existence. The government then attempted another purge, but international pressure stopped the persecutions. By 1917 the Japanese Christians had so flourished that they had built the massive St. Mary's Cathedral in Nagasaki. The chaplain had said he was afraid that what Japanese Imperialism couldn't do in 200 years of persecution, we had done in seconds with our atomic bomb.

How is it, I thought, when I should be feeling jubilant about the war being over and looking forward to going home, I have such contradictory feeling about it all? Is this victory part of something good, or part of something evil? We were told that on the day when the first atomic bomb was dropped on August 6th, President Truman, aboard the battle cruiser Augusta, turned to a group of sailors nearby, and said, "This is the greatest thing in history." Was it? Most of the men around me thought it was, and they had few misgivings about the bomb. And then a second bomb. Had it been necessary? Or was this a sign that we had lost the will to resist evil, an admission that we had lost the moral capacity to distinguish between right and wrong.

Within days the crew was informed that the final Peace Surrender would be signed aboard the Missouri. On August 27 the Missouri dropped anchor in a Japanese port not far from Tokyo, and five Japanese were taken on board to help arrange for the Surrender events. On the 29th the ship moved into Tokyo Bay itself. I was amazed to see damaged warships and the vast destruction in the city, which I could see through binoculars. Also, I was amazed to see so many other American ships in the Bay. Later I was to learn that one of my brothers-in-law was on an oil tanker only a few hundred yards distant, though he was unable to visit or signal me.

Finally the big day of Sunday, September 2, 1945 arrived, the day for signing the Instrument of Surrender, bringing the fighting between Japan and the allied nations to a formal close. I was thrilled to be part of the Honor Guard that day, the third man in the first row, 15 feet from where the Japanese Foreign Minister of Japan, Mr. Mamoru Shigemitsu, came aboard, together with other emissaries, to sign the historic document. One of my Marine buddies had the honor of stepping forward to frisk the Foreign Minister and the other Japanese emissaries, to ensure that they were not armed.

The various news and cameramen of each country all had their assigned locations. The presence of the Russian cameramen, whose station was directly behind the Honor Guard, was one of the interesting sidelights of the day for me. Anxious to get the best possible pictures for their cameras, they kept crowding us Marines, until finally we were ordered to hold them back. Although none of them spoke English, as far as I could tell, their laughing and behavior was typical of what any Americans would have been doing on such a job. I remembered that when I had been in high school, the common view was that the 'communists' were the real threat to all peace loving and democratic peoples. Then suddenly the Russians had become our allies in the war, and the Japanese became known as the vile and evil peoples. Now, in this first direct encounter that I had with Russian people, they appeared indistinguishable from Americans, except for their language. In fact, our exchange with them was almost playful. In contrast to this, at the time, both the French and English TV crews were uncooperative in comparison.

The ceremonies took place on the gallery deck on the starboard side of the ship, about 25 feet from where I in the Honor Guard stood. At 0800 o'clock Admiral of the Fleet Chester W. Nimitz arrived on board with his staff, followed by other high-ranking Army and Navy and Marine officers. At 0830 representatives of the Allied Powers began coming aboard, representing the United Kingdom, China, USSR, Australia, Canada, France, New Zealand, and the Netherlands. At 0855 the Japanese delegation, headed by Foreign Minister Shigemitsu, came aboard and mounted the gallery deck to take their positions before the green cloth covered mess table, which had been brought up from the mess-hall at the last moment. Behind the table were all the representatives of the Allied Powers. Promptly at 0900, General Douglas MacArthur, Supreme Commander for the Allied Powers, came from the Admiral's cabin and took his position in front of a battery of microphones, to accept the surrender of Japan on behalf of the Allied Powers.

Before the Japanese were invited to sign the Instrument of Surrender, General MacArthur stated the purpose of the occasion and an expression of hope for the future:

"It is my earnest hope—indeed the hope of all mankind—that from this solemn occasion a better world shall emerge out of the blood and carnage of the past, a world founded upon faith and understanding, a world dedicated to the dignity of man and the fulfillment of his most cherished wish for freedom, tolerance and justice."

At the conclusion of his speech, General MacArthur requested the Japan representatives to advance to sign the 'Instrument of Surrender' document. It read:

"We, acting by command of and in behalf of the Emperor of Japan, the Japanese Government and the Japanese Imperial General Headquarters, hereby accept the provisions set forth in the declaration issued by the heads of the Governments of the United States, China and Great Britain on the 26 July 1945, at Potsdam, and subsequently adhered to by the Union of Soviet Socialist Republics, which four powers are hereafter referred to as the Allied Powers. We hereby proclaim the unconditional surrender to the Allied Powers."

Then General MacArthur signed for the Allied Powers collectively, after which other representatives signed for their countries. It was a highly moving moment when General Jonathan Wainwright was asked to stand beside MacArthur as he signed the document. Wainwright had carried the fight for Corregidor in the Philippines to its bitter conclusion in 1942, and then taken prisoner and kept in a Japanese prisoner of war camp for three years before being released only a few days earlier. The first pen MacArthur used in affixing his signature was given to General Wainwright. The second pen used was given to General Percival, Commanding the British garrison at Singapore when it fell. After General MacArthur had signed, the representatives of the various Allied nations signed, Admiral Nimitz for the United States, and then the others. MacArthur then announced that it was his purpose to see to it that the terms of surrender were carried out. The Japanese then stepped forward to receive their copy of the surrender documents, and then left the ship.

After the ceremony was completed, MacArthur broadcasted the following message to the American people (in part):

> "Today the guns are silent. A great tragedy has ended. A great victory has been won...the entire world lies quietly at peace. The holy mission has been completed. I look back on the long, tortuous trail from those grim days of Bataan and Corregidor, when an entire world lived in fear, when democracy was on the defensive everywhere, when modern civilization trembled in the balance, I thank a merciful God that he has given us the faith, the courage, and the power from which to mold victory. We have known the bitterness of defeat and the exultation of triumph, and from both we have learned there can be no turning back. We must go forward to preserve in peace what we won in war.
>
> A new era is upon us. Even the lesson of victory itself brings with it profound concern both for our future security and the survival of civilization. The destructiveness of the war potential, through progressive advances in scientific discovery, has in fact now reached a point, which revises the traditional concept of war.
>
> Men from the beginning of time have sought peace. Various methods through the ages have been attempted to devise an international process to prevent or settle disputes between nations. From the very start, workable methods were found insofar as individual citizens were concerned, but the mechanics of an instrumentality of larger international scope have never been successful. All in turn failed, leaving the only path to be by way of the crucible of war. The utter destructiveness of war now blots out this alternative. We have had our last chance. If we will not devise some greater and more equitable system, Armageddon will be at our door. The problem basically is theological and

involves a spiritual recrudescence and improvement of human character that will synchronize with our almost matchless advances in science, art, literature, and all material and cultural developments of the past 2000 years. It must also be of the spirit if we are to save the flesh."

The speech continued, though for me these words were to occupy my mind and heart for days. And not just for days, but for the rest of my life.

And so after 1364 days, 5 hours and 14 minutes, World War II, ended officially at 0904 September 2, 1945 with the signing of this 'Instrument of Surrender' on the battleship USS Missouri, anchored in Tokyo Bay.

On September 5 the Missouri left Tokyo Bay for Guam, Pearl Harbor, the Panama Canal, Norfolk in Virginia, and on Monday, October 22 had pulled into the Hudson River and Pier 90 in downtown New York, in time for Navy Day, 1945. It was not too long after this that I received my honorable discharge from the Marine Corps.

I had returned home to the States, a very different person than the one who had left it to join the fighting overseas. I was filled with pride in what had been accomplished by so many, especially those that had given so much more than I had given. How many dead? How many wounded? How many who would never be able to make up for what the years had cost them in love, in family, in health, in financial security, in memories of fighting, blood, and carnage?

My hope was that General MacArthur's hope of a better world emerging from all this would be realized. That peace would be preserved. That a new era had been born. That new international processes were being developed to prevent or to settle disputes between nations. That a spiritual recrudescence and improvement of human character would match the advances in science, art, literature, and all the material and cultural development of the past 2,000 years, and yes, the last 4 or 5 years, would be realized. This was my dream, my vision that I wanted to commit myself to, that a world of true peace, of real justice, of realistic democracy, and of loving community would become a living reality in the years ahead. Yes--- I would give myself to that dream

However, alongside this passionate hope was another strong and wearisome and confusing feeling. I had always considered myself a patriot. However I did not believe in the 'my country right or wrong' attitude that I had found so common, not only among my shipmates on board ship, but also among the officers I had encountered, including those in highest authority. The anti-Semitism that Rosen spoke about, confirmed in conversations among shipmates, and apparently part of our nations indifference to the blood bath of Jews in Europe evident in President Roosevelt's leadership and Congressional silence, and silence in our national media, were troubling for me. And were the Japanese really as barbarian and treacherous as Admiral Halsey had suggested? Tac, my schoolmate, surely wasn't. And was America the force of righteousness and decency that Halsey had claimed? It was my fellow Americans who had gone ashore in the Philippines and raped simple village women who were our allies in the glorious war we had been fighting. It was white shipmates who discriminated against my Negro friend George, and riled against me for befriending him. It was the angry black Reggie who had exposed the phony liberal so-called acceptance of their black fellow-citizen. Even my truth loving white teachers in high school and my teachers in Sunday school had failed to do that. And if Big Jim and Rusty were typical red-necks from the south who were racists, was it because they too were raised in poverty and competed with the Negro for their 'place in the sun', unlike northern liberals like myself who had never had to compete with people of other races? And after observing so much blatant heterosexual disregard of moral values, how could society, and even my own church and pastor, be so judgmental of homosexuals, especially of one like my friend Len, who was probably one of the most ethical men I had met in the Marine Corps?

Even more baffling to me was the almost complete silence while I was growing up regarding Christian teaching about pacifism and nonviolence and war. After all, I had grown up in a Christian family, had been active in my church, and yet I had never been faced with having to make a conscientious decision about going to war. If the teaching of Jesus was to "love your enemy" and to "overcome evil with good" and "not to return violence for violence", and which was what the Christian church practiced for its first 300 years, why hadn't I been told that? If 'conscientious objection' to participating in war was required of those who refused to go to war, why wasn't the 'conscientious choice to participate' in war required of those who chose to go to war? I could understand why the nation wouldn't require it, but I expected that the church should require it if the church was going to be faithful to the teachings of Jesus. And facing me was the question of where I would place my primary loyalty. Was it to my country, or to God? Who was I to obey, 'God or Man?' That was a question that had confronted me, and would continue to confront me, over and over again.

So now I'm going home. I've spent nearly three years in the Marine Corps, much of it overseas, fighting in a war to bring peace. What is peace? Is it just the cessation of warfare? Or is peace much more than that? When my grandfather died, I remember people saying at the funeral, after viewing the body, "He looks so peaceful." Peaceful? He looked dead to me, I thought. The absence of the war sure felt good to me. But was that the extent of peace? The question confronted me over and over again. And a certain resolve increasingly came to dominate my thoughts: I want to learn what real peace is? I want to study it, and work for it. I want to be a peacemaker!

But where will that resolve take me, I wondered? Perhaps a career in the military is the best way for me to work toward peacemaking. However, the more I pursued that option, the more I was convinced that, important as that option might be, it wasn't a satisfying answer. Perhaps teaching would be the best route, actually guiding young people toward a set of values that would make peace possible. Or psychology, understanding the inner workings that propel many to violence and others to constructive action. Or religion, enabling people to attune their lives to the source of life, grounding their lives in a right relationship with God and society. To be a pastor had a strong appeal to me also. Though maybe politics was a better route if I really wanted to make a difference. Unless people, and nations, learned to act in a civil manner to each other, living within the law, there could be no lasting peace.

And so I headed home, to my family, to get an education and to begin a career. After my service in the Marine Corps and fighting for peace, I was now determined to work for peace in a different way. Somehow or other, I felt that there must be a better way to achieve peace than through war. The costs of war were too high. War turned people into warriors, not peacemakers. Warfare sought 'ends' that were inconsistent with its 'means', and I was sure that the means must be consistent with the ends for a peaceful result. Somehow I felt that it was not peace that followed war, only the lull after the storm. The wreckage remained. No, I felt the way to real peace must itself be peaceful. Peace is the way, not just the goal, I reasoned. And so, heading home, I set off on the journey of peacemaking.

PART II:
THE JOURNEY – THE STORM ALONG THE WAY

This conjunction of an immense military establishment and a large arms industry is new in the American experience. We recognize the imperative need for this development. Yet we must not fail to comprehend its grave implications. We must guard against the acquisition of unwarranted influence, whether sought or unsought, by the military-industrial complex. The potential for the disastrous rise of misplaced power exists and will persist.

—President Dwight Eisenhower

Chapter 4

1945—1960: The Lull Before the Storm

FOR THE FIRST TWO weeks after arriving in New York from overseas the battleship Missouri was berthed at the prominent pier #90 in downtown New York. During this time the ship was open to the public for viewing, and thousands stood in long lines every day, especially to see the historic spot where the Peace Surrender Ceremonies had been signed at the end of the Second World War. The crowds came aboard the ship via the rear gangway, took a brief tour of the main deck and signing site, and left via the front gangway. The crew soon discovered that they could carefully survey the visitors and then, selecting the most interesting and usually good looking young women, offer to give them a specially guided extra tour to some of the other special spots on the ship. This often ended up with a date having been established for that evening or the next. You can be sure that I was no exception in taking advantage of this opportunity.

Marines in particular had it good in New York. Most returning veterans were either Army or Navy, having served in the European Theater, and therefore returned to the East Coast. The Marines, on the other hand, had mostly served in the Pacific Theater, and very few returned to the states via the East Coast and New York. The Service Centers and USOs treated all veterans to a wide selection of free entertainment, but with so few Marine veterans in the city, they had almost preferred status. Rosen, Len, Leroy and our pals and I had our pick of free opportunities. We went to football games, ice hockey and basketball games (baseball was not in season) as well as opera, Broadway theaters (among the current shows were 'Up in Central Park', 'Oklahoma', and 'Polonaise'), and big names bands like Tommy and Jimmy Dorsey and Harry James, banquets, dances, and other attractions galore. My $54 monthly pay wouldn't have gone very far normally, but all this was available to veterans freely in appreciation of their service time.

The USS Missouri after two weeks moved to dry dock at the Brooklyn Navy Yard for several months for repairs. My shipmates and I soon discovered a good use for the Wallet Sized Cards that they had given to us after the Surrender Ceremony in Tokyo. The card printed with the red and white colored Japanese Flag as background stated, "Certifying the Presence of PFC Jerry Pedersen (with my serial number), U.S. Marine Corps at the formal surrender of the Japanese Forces to the Allied Powers on Sept. 2, 1945, Tokyo Bay, USS Missouri," was good for free rounds of drinks when we showed it at any bar we entered. One of my favorite lines there was "yes, there we were at the signing of the Surrender Ceremonies in Tokyo Bay—General Douglas McArthur, Admirals Nimitz and Halsey, General Wainwright, and...of course...PFC Jerry Pedersen". It always got a good laugh, and another round of 'set em up for the boys'.

Earlier I had also seen a bit of the south when the Missouri docked at Norfolk Virginia. On liberty, after seeing the signs "colored only" and "whites only" over restroom and drinking faucets and playgrounds for children, I began to really understand what George, one of the Negro mess hands on board ship, had been saying regarding Negro attitudes about America. And only then could I begin to understand how Reggie, George's angry Negro friend, could say that he felt closer to the Japanese, whom America was fighting against, than to white Americans, who treated Negroes as inferior, second class citizens. My first reaction had been to feel ashamed for the southern whites, although I soon began having a sense of shame myself, as I realized that I and all white Americans benefited from the past slavery, and the continuing racial discrimination that the Negroes in America suffered. I wanted to protest against it somehow, but my buddies talked me out of it, saying it might make me feel better, but the local retribution to my protest would be taken out on the local Negro population. It was then that I remembered George's quoting Langston Hughes' poem— "What happens to a dream deferred? Does it dry up like a raisin in the sun?...Or does it explode?" I was convinced that this kind of evil and discrimination must rapidly begin changing for the better, or surely there would be an explosion in America. And I had to admit that I would be on the side of those pushing for rapid change.

The thrill of ending the war in Tokyo Bay at the Peace Surrender Signing aboard the USS Missouri on Sept. 2, 1945, and thrill of returning home to the States shortly after this, could be matched only by the thrill I enjoyed on March 17, 1946 when I finally received my Honorable Discharge from the United States Marine Corps at the Great Lakes Naval Training Station. I had hopes that peace was really becoming a world reality, especially in light of the founding of the United Nations in the preceding months. The process that had led finally to the United Nations began while I was still in high school, in June, 1941, when the representatives of ten nations fighting Nazi Germany met in London to agree on efforts to achieve world peace following the war in which they were then engaged. At that time the United States still had not entered the war, but by January 1, 1942 the US was not only in WWII but had signed the initial Declaration of United Nations. Toward the end of the war this led finally to the San Francisco Conference where fifty Nations began meeting on April 25, 1945. The conference began just thirteen days after President Franklin D. Roosevelt died, and twelve days before the Surrender of Germany, and four months before the surrender of Japan. By June 26, 1945 the Charter had been agreed to and signed by all fifty representatives, which then had to be approved by the five permanent members of the proposed Security Council (US, Britain, Soviet Union, France, and China) and a majority of the other member nations. Finally, on October 24, 1945, the United Nations became a reality.

Naturally, the final months of my service in the Marine Corps were filled with the excitement of the end of the war and the founding of the United Nations. However, just twelve days before I was to be discharged on March 17th, 1946, an event took place that began to make me wonder about the prospects of peace. Winston Churchill, Britain's leader throughout the war, made a speech at Fulton, Missouri, which was to become known as the 'Iron Curtain Speech'. In it he warned of danger to the West from the Soviet Union, and repudiated reliance on the old doctrine of the balance of power, which he labeled as unsound. He said: "We cannot afford to work on a narrow margin of power". Rather, he said: "The U.S. stood at the pinnacle of world power, and must remain the premier power in the world and must never allow anyone to be tempted to oppose us with a trial of strength". He said: "We had done our duty In overcoming the tyranny of the Axis Powers, but now we must feel anxiety, lest we fall and let down our guard". It was a 'call-to-arms'; it was an announcement of the onset of the Cold War.

As I completed my military service, I began to have serious doubts that we had brought to an end the violence of war. I remember wondering earlier after the second Atomic Bomb was dropped on Nagasaki, why had it been dropped? The rumors had already begun aboard ship that the war was drawing to a close. Now, I questioned, had the Bomb really signaled the beginning of the end of the war, or was it in reality the first military operation of the beginning cold war? Were we thinking that because we were victors in that war, that war really pays? Or that war was to be the first option to international problems rather than the last resort? Is what we were calling peace simply a brief interlude between wars? Had the 20 million Soviets who were killed during WWII taught the Soviets nothing? Had the millions of our Allies who were killed during WWII taught the allied nations nothing? Had these casualties during WWII taught us nothing? Was America going to treat the newly established United Nations with the same lack of respect that they had shown to the League of Nations following WWI? Would I ever really experience peace in this world?

To be home again was a happy time. Two of my brothers-in-law had returned from the Navy before me, as well as one from the Merchant Marines, all of them older than I, married, and with children. And I was so glad Mom and Dad had been able within the last two years to purchase the first home they had ever owned. It was small, but their two-bedroom bungalow was all they needed, and they were proud of it. After years feeling lucky just to have a job, much of the time earning eighteen dollars a week, which didn't go very far when they had been raising 4 children, they now felt elated. As a child I remembered my mom taking in washing and doing ironing to help pay the bills. It was good to see my mom now not having to labor so hard and enjoying herself. Although so many in the war had paid a terrible price, I realized that I was glad that some people like my folks had profited during the war.

Although I was pleased that my parents had actually improved their financial situation during the war, it came as a surprise to me that many others also seem to have benefited from wartime, and that a few had profited enormously. My dad had to work terribly hard and long hours at his taxi job, however it was the best income he had in his entire life, enabling him to save enough to buy a home for the first time, even though the home cost only $6,000. Although many of the immediate family members of service men had much financial strain caused by the war, many citizens ended the war better off than before. It was said that the depression years of the 1930s in America did not really end before 1941, rather only after the greater military spending of the war years.

I wondered—is it possible that the only way for a nation to end its economic depression is through war, through military spending? Is the threat of violence, the threat of enemies, necessary to motivate people to have the political will to appropriate the necessary moneys to improve societies economic problems? Were the appeals to sacrifice by civilians, like gas rationing, victory gardens and savings bonds, really only a rationalization to make people feel good about themselves and their improved living conditions despite the deaths, causalities, and carnage of war? I wondered—that even though tens of millions of people were killed in WWII, mostly civilians, and only a small minority of them Americans – is it possible that America would soon forget the tragedies of war as we had emerged from the that war as the world's most powerful nation? I wondered.

Later, soon after the war, my father reached retirement age, and was able to retire. He was fortunate that the Social Security Act had begun in the '30s, so that he became one of the early ones to be able to retire with a little income from it. It was the only income he would then have to live on, even though it was very small. Several years after retiring my father told me: "You'll never know how much my monthly social security means to me. When we sold our home and moved into the Trailer Park, Mom and I did pretty well for several years living entirely on our little savings and our social security. But when our saved money ran out, we could manage to live solely on our social security by being very careful. In the past the majority of seniors were among the poor, unless they were fortunate enough to live with their kids. It worked pretty well when people lived on farms, especially if they lived simply and grew their own food. But living in the city and being dependent on a car just doesn't work out once you no longer have that weekly paycheck. Without my social security check I'd be living in the Poor Farm— but you kids don't even know what that is because they don't have them anymore. Or, maybe we'd be lucky, and you kids would take us in to your homes. We are so thankful for that monthly S.S. check. I wonder if future generations will appreciate it, since they wouldn't have known about what elderly people faced in the old days."

I, for one, said I would never forget it, because I remembered uncles and aunts living under miserable conditions when I was a little boy, and now I too wondered if my kids and future generations would understand.

I soon discovered many of the more than seventeen million men and women who had put on the military uniform in WW II, ten million of whom had served overseas, had the same idea I had of going back to school. Undoubtedly much of the reason for the large number of enrollees in educational pursuits was due to the G.I. Bill. This Veterans Benefit Bill, established following the Second World War, enabled many men to go who might never have been able to go to college otherwise. Many of them, having matured greatly during their experience in the military, now saw the benefit of getting an education. Professors and administrators in colleges said that by bringing many older and mature men and women into colleges, the G.I. Bill had helped change the nature of higher education itself. These veterans, who had faced life and death situations in wartime, tended to be more serious about getting an education than had previous generations that had gone to college directly out of high school. I knew that this was true for me.

While serving in the Marine Corps as a PFC, I had been paid $54 a month, and had even been able to save some money on that amount while I was overseas. However, now as a civilian, I soon discovered that going to college full time, even with part time jobs, was financially difficult. I worked in service stations and coached sports for the school system, with the G.I. Bill was able to vigorously pursue my BA degree, and then after marriage, my` MA degree. Like many other married veterans, the $105 a month from the G.I. Bill for Education for living expenses, together with tuition and books, helped make this education possible. Undoubtedly, the G.I. Bill for Education was nothing short of revolutionary for veterans, and literally changed the nature of higher education following WWII.

Although I found my college studies interesting, much of it seemed distanced from 'life', from 'real life' and all the issues like those that I had experienced while overseas. I often remembered what my father had said about "college men" —they know a lot about book learning, but really don't know that much about the really important things in life. I also remembered what my friend Len had told me, that I had learned more from my reading and experiences in my time overseas than he had learned and experienced during his four years in college. I wasn't too sure about that, though I was sure that I had at least learned the questions to ask of life, to question authority and to challenge hypocrisy and falsehood whenever I encountered it.

As college graduation approached, I was confronted by my earlier decision to direct my life towards peacemaking. But how to do it? About this time I read a statement made by A.J. Muste of the Fellowship of Reconciliation— "There is no way to peace, Peace is the Way." If that were true, and due to my experiences I was sure it was true, then I knew that I must find a way to actually live the peaceable life, and encourage others to live that life, and be an advocate for a truly peaceful world.

My favorite Political Science prof. urged me to go into politics or international relations as a good way to promote peacemaking. A grad student, known as the college Marxist, urged me to go into the economic field, since he was sure economic determinism was what drove society to either peace or conflict. A Psychology prof. extolled the insights that psychology shed on peacemaking. And the reason I had selected Sociology as my major was primarily for this reason. The teaching field especially appealed to me, since I was convinced that youth experiences were crucial in forming one's life commitments. However, my own growing experience of a spirituality that centered in a profound sense of 'inner peace' while at the same time demanding the search for 'outer peace' for the world, led me to the field of religion.

I seriously tried to analyze how 'peace' had come to be so central for me in my journey through life. I was sure that growing up with strong family solidarity and security was a major factor in my sense of 'inner peace' that had carried me through my years of military life and college education. Also, my religious foundations growing up in a Lutheran Church further enhanced this sense of 'inner peace'. The strength of that experience was the emphasis on the grace and love of God for us. The message I had continually received was that God loved us and accepted us as a free and undeserved gift to us. Unlike some of my friends, I had never had to struggle or search to find God or to be at peace with God, rather God found me and gave me a peace within. We were only to give thanks for this gift of acceptance and peace that God gives us, which we know through Jesus Christ. This was the basis of my 'inner peace'.

However, it bothered me that my Lutheran Church experience had little to say about the 'outer peace' which was the goal of my peacemaking. For instance, it was only as I studied history that I had learned that the Lutheran Church in Germany had been largely silent as Hitler came to power and led his nation to the violence of the Holocaust and WWII. The church historically had kept silent about government and politics because of what it called the *Two Kingdoms* teaching, which taught that the church had authority and represented God for spiritual matters and that governments had authority and represented God in secular matters. The church, having abandoned its prophetic and critical function regarding Hitler, soon discovered that many Germans accepted the Nazi idea that Hitler spoke for God, and Hitler soon displaced for most Germans the church's authority even in the spiritual realm. Likewise, while growing up I had never heard that for the first three centuries Christians had refused to 'serve in the military', or the teachings of Jesus about nonviolence. Religion and Faith had been presented as largely a private matter, with only minor attention to social, political and public matters. It was with this tension between the 'inner' and 'outer' understanding of religion and spirituality that I set out for graduate school.

Though first I got married. I had entered the Marine Corps expecting to find romance and meet my Maureen O'Hara like the one in the motion picture 'To the Shores of Tripoli', but I never found either the romance or the girl while in the Marine Corps. Returning home, I soon found both the romance and the girl. Although I had been determined to 'play the field' when I got home, I quickly changed my mind. After meeting my dream-girl, Dru, the other girls I dated had no appeal. As I approached graduation from college, I asked this dream-girl to marry me. Little did I realize how important this was to become in my journey through life, contributing to my experience of actually living 'in peace' as I searched 'for peace' and for striving to be a peacemaker.

Many years later I wrote in a book that I had given to this dream-girl, Dru, who had become my wife: "To the woman to whom men are first attracted to for her beauty— and then amazed by her wisdom— and women find a close and dear friend; from Jerry, who was first attracted by her beauty and then amazed by her wisdom – and still is!" And I have often told her, and everyone else, that the best and smartest and most rewarding thing that I had ever done in my life was to ask her to marry me. She has shared my dreams, my struggles, my adventures, and my love.

Immediately after college graduation and getting married, we took off to the East Coast to study at a Theological Seminary.

During that first year, the month of January offered a time of individual study, and I selected to research the American church's history regarding Labor Unions and Marxism. My faculty advisor and other faculty discouraged my doing this, suggesting that I do something more 'religiously significant'. I argued that I thought this had great 'religious significance' and that it had grown out of my desire to be a peacemaker. I had been reading Toynbee's '*A Study of History*' and E.S. Jones '*Christ's Alternative to Communism*' and argued that what was developing in the Soviet Union was nothing less than a new quasi-religion. Toynbee had argued that Marxism was being converted into a substitute for Christianity; Marx being its 'Moses' and Lenin its 'Messiah', with '*The Communist Manifesto*' and other writings being their 'Sacred Scripture'. I argued that we needed to better understand Marxism and its appeal, so as to counter its attraction, if we thought it was wrong. Further, and what really bothered some of my advisors, was that I suggested that if we really wanted to oppose the Communist agenda, we had better begin a more serious presentation of Jesus' announcement that "the Kingdom of God is at hand" and what it demanded of us in America for the twentieth century.

It further surprised and disappointed me to learn that my church had strongly opposed the development of Labor Unions throughout our history in America. During my summer and part-time employment while in college I had been a short-term member of three different labor unions at a Ford assembly plant, a lumber mill, and a meat packing plant. Compared to the very minimum wages I had earned working in service stations, coaching, and other non-union labor jobs, the union jobs, although all were doing manual labor, had offered me a job with a wage, dignity and respect that I felt every worker should have. The month-long research experience was so discouraging that I nearly decided to leave Seminary and begin searching for another vocation. However, immediately after this month of research, I was able to attend an inter-seminary conference with students and faculties from many different religious faiths. One of the speakers, who happened to be a faculty member of another school of my same denomination, spoke about the important role of Labor Unions in helping to bring justice to the slugfest between labor and management in this country. He also spoke about the splits and divisions between nations, classes, races, and religions, saying we live in a world of undeclared wars, methodical violence, political aggression and moral disintegration. He said that fear drives us to the false security of force and violence. He said we must address this chaos, and it was to this task that we were being called. Wow, I thought—let me at it!

Following this experience, I decided to continue in my studies and preparation in the field of religion, that it might become a source of hope, rather than a contributor to despair—or in my terms, contribute to 'outer peace' as well as 'inner peace.'

The remaining years of the 1950s went fast. Internationally, the new communist government in China, the Korean War, the beginnings of our involvement in Vietnam and in Central and South America were disturbing developments, but the conceptualizing and execution of the Marshall Plan was a magnificent effort toward a peaceful world. Personally, the years led to my Masters Degree, my ordination as a pastor, and starting a new congregation with all its community involvement and relationships.

One incident stands out strong in my early years as a minister that occurred at one of the first Synod Conferences I attended. The proposal was made that all ministers should be provided medical health insurance. Much discussion took place regarding the costs of the plan and other details. Finally, I took the mike to speak against the proposal, making it clear that that I was not against health insurance, rather that I wanted it for 'all people', not just ministers. I warned that once we were protected, we would be tempted to forget about those who were not protected, the vast majority of all people. Our prophetic role was to speak out about injustices in our society, and especially to speak out on behalf of those who had little voice in public affairs, especially the poor. It would be so easy, once we were protected, to forget the needs of those who weren't. My objections were totally ignored—in fact I doubt that few even 'heard' them, so satisfied that their own needs were being met. I remember it as the first strong impression made on me that ministers were not much different than most people. Most ministers see themselves, as 'pastors', not 'prophets'—as 'shepherds for their sheep', not 'watchdogs for society'. I was becoming aware that my 'quest for peace' required a 'quest for justice' as well.

Perhaps the most important lesson I had to learn in my early pastoral experience was that people are very slow about accepting new ideas and putting them into practice. I had expected this in the wider community, but was surprised that it was true to a large extent also among people of faith. Even then, older and more experienced pastors kept telling me that I was far more successful in this than most. To the degree this was true, my conclusion was that this resulted for two reasons. First, I determined to be relentless in speaking and acting continually for peace and justice, whereas I felt many other ministers that I observed really didn't. And second, I always made sure that people understood that my advocacy for peace and justice was an expression of our faith. Often I would hear the complaint about my being too 'political', whereas I was insistent that these were 'spiritual' matters, based on the Bible, and simply 'following Jesus.' I insisted that any spirituality that didn't have profound political, social and ethical implications simply would be false spirituality.

Further graduate studies led to reception of my Doctorate Degree, followed by a professorship in a seminary. Best of all was the thrill of a happy marriage and an enlarging family with the birth of my son, Brad, and my daughter, Kim. My joys were beyond number. And yet, I still knew that something was missing in the adventure of my continuing journey, especially in the journey of peacemaking.

As the decade of the 1950s came to an end, I read the final speech that the outgoing President of the United States, General Dwight Eisenhower, gave before leaving office. I discovered that he shared some of the same concerns that I had, especially my fears regarding the future of peace. President Eisenhower said he had to confess that as he ended his fifty years of serving his country in war and in the presidency, he had a deep sense of disappointment. He knew the horrors of war, and he had hoped to be able to report that a lasting peace was in sight. However, the best he could say was that during his years in office, war had been avoided. However, he warned that too many people were tempted to believe that some spectacular military action could miraculously solve all of our difficulties. He said he recognized the need for a strong military establishment so that no potential aggressor would be tempted to risk their own destruction. However, the President warned against "the dangers of the unwarranted influence of the military/industrial complex" that had only come into existence following WWII, and especially during his eight years in office. He said: "peace can only come when the world, ever growing smaller, avoids becoming full of fear and hate and instead lives as one community of mutual trust and respect". And he emphasized that this one world community must insure that even the weakest members are honored, respected and protected as fully as we are by our moral, economic and military strength.

As we approached the new decade of the 1960s, I should have been elated that my concerns were also the concerns of our famous General and President, but I wasn't. I realized more than ever that my hopes for peace were not well founded, and my fears were very realistic. We were no nearer peace now fourteen years after the end of WWII than we were back then. Perhaps we were further from a peaceful world. Now we were engaged in a Cold War that seemed to have no end, with the threat of nuclear war a real possibility. Earlier I took comfort in the fact that only our nation possessed the capacity for using nuclear weapons, but now another powerful nation had that capacity also, and who knew how many others might soon achieve it. Eisenhower had confirmed that our massive arms industry, which had hardly existed when he came into office, was now a potential threat to the very structure of our society. President Eisenhower stated that until peoples of all faiths, all races, and all nations had their basic human needs satisfied, and that until the scourges of poverty, disease and ignorance were eliminated, the hope of peoples living together in a peace guaranteed by the binding force of mutual respect and love would not be achieved.

Jerry Pedersen

As I prepared to enter this decade of the '60s, I determined to seriously pursue the path of peacemaking. I decided that I could best achieve that in a university setting. I was hopeful and confident that college-aged students were open and teachable, necessary qualities if we were to achieve our goal of peace. I was hopeful that the academic environment of inquiry and truth seeking would work in the interest of peacemaking.

"Finally, to those who would make themselves our adversary, we offer not a pledge but a request: that we both begin anew the quest for peace, before the dark powers of destruction unleashed by science engulf all humanity in planned or accidental self-destruction."

— John F. Kennedy

PEDERSEN FAMILY
WITH PROFESSOR AT
UNIVERSITY

PEDERSEN AND HIS
TANZANIAN
REPLACEMENT
AFTER 3 YEARS
(LEFT)

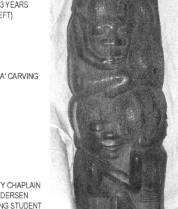

'UJAMAA' CARVING

UNIVERSITY CHAPLAIN
DR. PEDERSEN
COUNSELING STUDENT
(LEFT)

JERRY
TALKING WITH
PROFESSOR
AND
STUDENTS IN
DAR ES
SALAAM,
TANZANIA

56

Chapter 5

1960s: The Storm Builds—A Global View

MY OPTIMISM FOR A more peaceful world took a gigantic leap forward at the beginning of the decade of the '60s with the inauguration of John F. Kennedy on January 20, 1961. He expressed my hopes when he said that he "represented a new generation of leadership, one born in this century, one tempered by war, disciplined by a bitter peace and committed to human rights." I wanted to cheer when he requested our adversaries to join us in the quest for peace. He said our common enemies were tyranny, poverty, disease and war itself—and to rid ourselves of these enemies we must begin anew. And then in a ringing challenge, he asked us "not to ask what our country can do for us, but to ask what we can do for our country." I had been asking that question for fifteen years, and I was ready to recommit myself to that task.

However, within months I began being disillusioned of my hope of progress toward peace. We had been asked to 'begin anew' the task of our 'new generation' in a 'quest of peace'. What was revealed was continuation of the same old game of warmanship. We had pushed the Organization of American States to adopt the policy, which we then signed, which stated, "No state has the right to intervene in the internal affairs of another". JFK had affirmed this policy, boldly declaring on April 12th "we would not intervene in Cuba". We had been aware that the CIA, during the last years of the Eisenhower's presidency, had been seeking to undermine the new government of Fidel Castro in Cuba. However, we were not aware that the CIA was funding and training a group of Cuban exiles to invade Cuba to overthrow him. On April 17th the Bay of Pigs invasion by these CIA trained exiles began, only to be totally crushed within three days. No popular uprising against Fidel Castro took place, as the CIA had expected. In fact, we had helped organize and fund the invasion, and although the invading force was composed of exiles, there were some American planes and pilots used. Little did I realize that an explosive storm was on the horizon for our country. In fact, the storm had been gathering momentum for a long time.

The Cuban aspect of the storm climaxed in the October Crisis of 1962, the following year. It brought the possibility of war with the Soviets, a war that could have been nuclear. By this time I had become a Campus Pastor at Portland State University in Oregon. During the week leading up to October 28th students and faculty gathered at our campus ministry center, Koinonia House, to watch the crisis on TV as it developed. During that week everyone had become aware that the Soviets were shipping missiles with nuclear warheads to Cuba. Kennedy had warned that we would not tolerate the installation of missiles in Cuba. We understood that Soviet medium-range missiles had already been installed in Cuba, and that they were operational and probably armed with nuclear warheads. Kennedy had drawn a quarantine line which Soviets ships bound for Cuba must not pass beyond. On Wednesday, Oct. 24th, we watched, as were people all over the United States and the World, as our surveillance planes showed photographs of their ships approaching that quarantine line. Suddenly the Soviet ships stopped, and turned back. Had they not stopped we were told that our U.S. ships and planes would have forcibly stopped them. Undoubtedly this would then have been interpreted as an act of war, followed by a Soviet response and unpredictable rounds of escalation.

This was the first time that a confrontation like this between the only two great powers was simultaneously observed live on TV as it was happening. Everyone feared that this could be the beginning of WWIII, and the beginning of nuclear warfare. Existentially, it was like being present at the beginning of Creation itself, or, rather Armageddon. It was the first time Koinonia House, out of which our Ecumenical Ministry at PSU operated, was filled during much of the week with students and faculty from the campus. It was the first time I had seen 'fear' on their faces. Prayers had suddenly become very popular. I even saw the well-known faculty agnostic in a prayerful mood. I didn't know whether the prayers were addressed to God or to Kennedy or to Khrushchev, but I know it was one of the few existential moments... and hours... that I had up to this time lived through.

At the time, many students, and even some faculty, argued that the Cubans had no right to have missiles with nuclear warhead capable of being loosed over our country. And 'those Russians' were called belligerent, militaristic warmongers for trying to arm Cuba in this way. When I reminded them that we had missiles in Turkey and Italy, and military bases in all parts of the world surrounding the Soviets, and we claimed the legal and ethical right to do so to 'defend' our own country, my loyalty and patriotism as an American was questioned. One faculty member implied that I should stick to spiritual matters, and leave these political and secular matters to people who knew what they were doing. I began hearing from several congregations that were contributors to our financial support, threatening to discontinue their support and to have me removed from my position as campus pastor. Fortunately, many congregations, the entire ecumenical staff and the majority of students and faculty encouraged what we were doing as we suggested surely all nations had the same rights that we had and that this was a matter with which the United Nations should be involved. We continued supporting those who worked to counter nuclear proliferation, to begin armament reductions, and controlling the military/industrial complex that President Eisenhower had warned us about. We believed these were all ethical matters deeply related to spiritual concerns.

I had hoped that Kennedy, who had personified youth and vigor, would symbolize that the moment of change for the quest for peace would become a reality for America. Up to this point, my hopes for peace had not been completely dashed by Eisenhower's warning of the Military/Industrial Complex, followed by the Bay of Pigs and the October Crisis. However, my hopes for the quest for peace were nearly dashed the following year on Friday, Nov. 22nd, 1963 when Kennedy was assassinated in Dallas, Texas. Within moments of the news of the shooting, our Campus Ministry Center was again filled with students and faculty. If 'fears' had dominated their faces at the October Crisis a year earlier, it was 'tears' that dominated their faces this time. Beautiful dreams and hopes were shattered by the violence of the day. First President Kennedy had been shot about 12:30 noon, wife Jackie at his side, and Texas Governor John Connally wounded, then the announcement from the hospital at 1:33 that Kennedy had died. Vice President Lyndon Johnson was soon sworn in at 2:38 as President aboard the President's plane headed for the Capitol, with Jackie at his side with her husband's blood on her suit and stockings. On Saturday Vigil was kept in the East Room of the White House. On Sunday a procession went from the East Room to the Rotunda at the Capital, where over 250,000 people passed by the bier before the following day. Then again on Monday, the national day of mourning, a procession went to St. Matthew's Cathedral for Mass, and then on to Arlington Cemetery.

All this was taking place live before our eyes on TV, interspersed with photos of Lee Harvey Oswald being arrested even before the new president was sworn in. This was followed on Sunday morning with an audience of many millions of people watching on TV as Oswald was being transferred from the city prison to the county jail, when suddenly Jack Ruby, owner of a local strip-tease joint, shot him. Now, not only had two shootings happened live before our eyes, but also everything in the Capitol the following days before thousands of people, including kings, presidents, prime ministers and leaders from nearly every country in the world, and millions of viewers on TV. For me, as for most people, these four days were a once-in-a lifetime dismal experience.

What did all this mean? We had known the exhilaration of a vigorous young president challenging both our nation and our potential opponents to move forward in the quest for peace! Unfortunately we then watched as he and our nation continued a foreign policy that demanded rights for ourselves that we denied to others, specifically at the Bay of Pigs and in the October Crisis, with its threat of nuclear war. And now the killing of the president. I wondered, is the Quest for

Peace really at the heart of being American, or is Violence really at the heart of being American, violence, which is as American as mom's apple pie? Is America best served by putting our national interest above the common good of other nations? Or is America better served when it puts the interest for peace in our own land alongside securing it for others as well? Is it possible for a person, or a nation, to live in peace when the society and world around it is in chaos? Yes, the question I found myself asking over and over, how can we succeed in this Quest for Peace?

During this time I was trying to discover how to do 'ministry' on a college campus. I did the usual things expected of me: teaching occasionally in classes and leading discussions on religion and ethics and conducting regular worship services. However I soon realized the limitations of such an approach. It soon became obvious that students, most of whom still lived at home while attending this commuter college, were confronting a new world for them, a world that challenged the pat answers they had too often absorbed from childhood and home and church. I found myself spending much of my time trying to free them from concepts and beliefs and attitudes that were at best inadequate, and often downright wrong. Naturally, this led to some conflict with a few parents and aggressive opposition from a few pastors. One parent complained: "I sent my son off to college, expecting him to finally come home with his values and faith unshaken – now he's changed." When I responded "hooray, growth is supposed to happen with higher education," she called for an investigation of my ministry. Another parent said that she was happy that at another college "My daughter went off to college and after four years came home unchanged."And I felt "what a failure!"

I was fortunate to have many excellent supporters on my PSU Ecumenical Ministry Board, among professors, local clergy, parents and students. One local pastor, Hal Sigmar, especially stands out. He was one of those all too rare people who deeply respect traditions and faith, even while seriously questioning them, reinterpreting them, and adapting them to an ever-changing world. Sigmar truly exemplified the saying: "Don't be an 'uncritical lover' or an 'unloving critic', but be a 'loving critic'." He was an accepting and affirming person, encouraging me to question, to be creative, to dare to act on my convictions and even to celebrate failure if it resulted from creative effort. Not only was he a model for me, but his wife Ethel, who shared his outlook and enjoyed and laughed at some of our foolish ways, was also a model for my wife and I. My relationship with him has never ended, and dialogue with him continues constantly, if not with him physically present, at least in my mind.

It was Hal who talked me into traveling with him to a lecture series in San Francisco featuring Paul Tillich, who had been a chief contributor to my doctoral dissertation five years earlier. Tillich introduced me to the term '*Kairos*', a special concept of time, to be differentiated from the concept of '*Chronos*' time. 'Chronos' is time as we observe it from moment to moment and day to day, linear time as we see it ticked off on the clock. 'Kairos' time however is not clock time, but a time of critical importance, a time when truth must be faced, a moment of judgment, a moment of grace and opportunity, a time when God issues a challenge to make critical decisions and take decisive action.

Tillich told of his 'Personal Kairos' and Germany's 'National Kairos' that occurred following the First World War in the relationship between the Socialist Movement and the Lutheran Church in Germany. Tillich participated in both of these. The Socialist Movement of which he was a part believed in the utopian hope of the coming in the near future of a thoroughly socialist or classless society. On the other hand, the Lutheran Church in Germany, of which he was a pastor, was not particularly interested in history at all, instead primarily interested in saving individuals from an evil world and believing true social change in society was impossible. Tillich tried to deal with the gap between these two views, the unrealistic utopian hopes of the socialists and the hopelessly conservative transcendental attitude of the Lutherans, seeing this as Germany's historical moment of 'Kairos'. It had been Germany's opportunity to affirm a new vision for the nation, by giving Socialism a new depth with a realistic religious dimension and Lutheranism a new depth with a realistic incarnational dimension. Germany's failure to do this resulted finally in the rise of the Nazi era and World War II.

This concept of 'Kairos' was to become for me important in my quest for peace. Without doubt, my 'Personal Kairos' was the repeated depths and highs in my life-— my despair at the dropping of the Atomic bombs in August and then the hopes of the Peace Surrender Signing in September of 1945— the continuing of my highs and lows with the Marshall Plan and then the Korean War—the Cold War and then Eisenhower's Warning—the Missile Crisis between Cuba/Russia/ America and Kennedy's Quest for Peace. I began asking the question: Is our nation on the road to a National Kairos Moment?

It was in the midst of pondering these questions that I had the opportunity to meet and converse with Martin Luther King, Jr. during my last year at PSU in 1963-4. He had recently given the 'I have a Dream' speech in the Washington DC rally. This was followed just 18 days later with the black Birmingham church bombing in which four girls were killed. I, of course, had followed the earlier development of black issues in civil rights. As a parish pastor I had supported the 1954 Supreme Court ruling against the 'separate but equal' doctrine that had such devastating effects on black citizens. I had applauded in 1955 and 56 when Rosa Parks refused to give up her seat on the bus in Montgomery, Alabama, and then supported the boycott of city buses, and condemned the bombing of four Negro churches and the bombing of Dr. King's home. As a seminary professor in February 1960, I had taken a strong stand of support for the students who sat down in the Woolworth lunch counter in Greensboro, North Carolina, and the spreading sit-ins that followed, which opened lunch counters in the south. And when Dr. King came to our campus at PSU, having been invited by our student government and one of our campus ministers Dick Gray, I was highly sympathetic to his witness to nonviolence and the strategy of nonviolent direct action.

Following Dr. King's speech I had the opportunity, together with a small group of interested people, to meet for a short time with him. I had opportunity to express my appreciation for his address, and all his previous leadership and action. I will never forget the thrust of his words as Dr. King looked at each of us, including me, eye to eye, saying: "I'm tired of people standing on the sidelines mouthing pious irrelevancies and sanctimonious trivialities, all the while living a life adjusted to the status quo. Especially you pastors, of all people, should know that Jesus disturbed the peace. He was an extremist. Don't be like so many luke-warm Christians. Be an extremist—but choose to be an extremist for love, not an extremist for hate. You're either an extremist for the cause of justice, or an extremist for the preservation of injustice." I went home and read again his 'Letter from the Birmingham Jail.'

Dr. King's words addressed to all of us, made a deep impression on me. I didn't feel they were words of judgment, but rather an appeal to my heart and mind, a call to rise up and act. It was a 'ah-ha' existential experience, a kind of conversion experience, a born-again experience, a 'wake up and live, stop talking and start acting, listen to your heart and respond with your hands and feet' call to get serious about my Journey of Peace Making.

A new direction for that journey soon became apparent. Hearing of an opening at the newly opening University College in Dar es Salaam, Tanganyika, Africa, I soon applied and was accepted for the position. In my resignation letter in the summer of 1964 to the national agency that had called me to Portland State University, I wrote, among other things:

> "Lately, as I have been evaluating my own situation, and as I contemplate the tumultuous, evolving, emerging, revolutionary developments in Africa, everything has been tapping me on the shoulder and saying 'go'. I feel that in many respects I am at a crossroads in my life. In no sense am I satisfied with my ministry to date. Cries for unleashing the power of redemptive-community have been allowed to be snuffed out by cowardice in the face of church-as-usual demands by those who have no sight, and self-awareness of my own inadequacies have too often blinded me to the hollowness of much campus intellectualism and the bravado of existing

power structures in both college and church. But so far I've been unable to effectively burst-out in imaginative action and creative leadership, which in my guts I feel I'm capable of doing. Hell, we've got plenty of mediocrity (and I thank God for the many who diligently carry on keeping wheels turning and the machinery oiled), but damn it, somehow I just can't be content to drift, to win the prizes handed out for those who agree not to rock the boat. Perhaps the secrets of God, for me, might be revealed in the hunger, suffering, and birth-paining aches of emerging Africa. I've tasted the best of being an educated man, I'm thoroughly at home as a secular man; yet, my life is utterly caught up in the cosmic unity of all things, grounded in the purposefulness of all existence, my perspective on life is completely formed and transformed by the life of the man Jesus, so much so that I want to share this perspective with everyone. And so Africa calls!"

Shortly before taking off for Africa, my wife and I traded off reading Robert Ruark's two books 'Something of Value' and 'Uhuru', books about the 'Mau Mau Emergency' in Kenya, East Africa in the 50s shortly before we headed for Africa. It scared the living daylights out of us. 'Uhuru' was a new word for us, which meant 'freedom' or 'a reign of terror', depending upon whether you were an African or a white settler in colonial East Africa at that time. For the large African majority, 'uhuru' meant freedom in a new Africa; a Utopia freed of colonial rule, revival of traditional African culture, and accessible land, which had been taken over by white settlers. For the much smaller minority of white settlers, 'uhuru' meant a threat to their white women, loss of their hard earned white property which they had toiled over with their back breaking efforts to clear the land, and their privilege of being white *Bwanas* over a less civilized suppressed black race. Reading Ruark's books, it sounded as though any white person present during this turmoil had lived in danger of losing their life. The fact that the Emergency had ended a few years before our arrival didn't bring us much comfort.

Jerry Pedersen

As we arrived in Nairobi for a short layover before flying on the next day to Dar es Salaam, I had the opportunity to discuss Ruark's books with several old-timers who had lived through the experiences Ruark had described. Their comments were later confirmed by my own studies and by Kenyan students and university faculty in Dar. Although many of the fears that whites had experienced were accurate, as were the intense anger of many Africans, the situation had been greatly exaggerated. Such fears had been perpetuated by the media and by circulation of local rumors, and by government colonial policy set overseas in Britain and enforced locally by self-serving local colonial officials. Further, the so-called savagery of Komo Kenyatta and other Kikuyu leaders were actually the actions of politically astute and cultured gentlemen who pursued the only path available to them toward achieving African rights and independence. Kenyatta had gone to England in 1929 with other Kikuyu representatives to plead for protecting African rights, had lived in England for many years over the next twenty years, and studied at the London School of Economics, where I would later spend a year of study and research. Back in Kenya, he had been arrested in 1952 as a Mau Mau leader and imprisoned for seven years during the Emergency. After being released from prison, he led the process of ending colonial rule in Kenya, and by the time I arrived in Africa he had become Prime Minister of the newly established independent nation of Kenya that had been established in 1963. Finally, on December 12, 1964, a short time after my arrival in Africa, he would become the President of the Republic of Kenya, a member of the British Commonwealth of Nations, and one of the most respected leaders in all of Africa.

This, my first encounter with African reality, set off for me further consideration of my ongoing search and quest for peace, and how best to achieve it. Objection by Africans to colonial rule, the desire for self-determination and independence, and resentment toward foreigners ignoring and destroying their culture, was understandable. Conflict in such circumstances was inevitable. Obviously, conflict was not the problem. Rather conflict was symptomatic of basic injustices existing in the colonial situation. The basic problem was refusing to acknowledge the injustice, and trying to maintain the unjust conditions of the status quo. Then, the use of force to maintain this unjust situation, especially using police and military force even though it was established by the existing governing authorities and therefore seemingly legal, was an inappropriate, unwise and ineffective solution to the problem. On the other hand, the anger generated by cultural disruption and the desire for independence from colonial rule on the part of the African people was not only understandable, it was also justified, although the violence of the rebellion can be questioned. The African militant response, and from a Western point of view a response that sometimes seemed extremely savage, was predictable and effective, in that it eventually led to the achievement of independence.

Surely there must have been a better way to achieve Independence. Might it have been possible to achieve Independence in a nonviolent way? Is the use of violence by those who suffer injustice justifiable in order to change the situation? If it is not wise, ethical, or responsible to use force to maintain the benefits and privileges of those who hold power in an unjust situation, what are the wise, ethical and responsible options? I began to realize that these are the questions that I must be ready to answer in my quest for peace.

I was filled with excitement as we headed for Dar es Salaam (Harbor or Haven of Peace), Tanganyika the next day. We stepped off the plane into the terrific heat along the Indian Ocean and were told that we were fortunate to have arrived on one of the more moderate days. We were taken to the New Africa Hotel, a relic from the earlier German Colonial Period from about 1890. It had open windows with no glass, but bars for safety, and ceiling fans for comfort. At night we would climb under mosquito nets covering our cots, thankful for that protection from the hated mosquito. I was relieved to learn that we had arrived during one of the two short hot seasons, between the two much cooler heavy rainy seasons. Within days I started wearing short pants and loose short sleeve shirts like everyone else, African and White.

The new campus for the University of East Africa was located eight miles out of town. Three years earlier one of the first decisions the new President Julius Nyerere made when Tanganyika became an independent nation in 1961 following the British colonial era, was to establish the first and only University in the country.

Nyerere believed that the nation could no longer afford to send its brightest students overseas for their education where many of the students remained permanently, having become accustomed to the favorable living conditions in the advanced industrial nations. And those who had returned to their homeland had become so accustomed to western culture and foreign standards that they wanted to continue them when they returned, contributing to the destruction of African culture and values. Although it would have actually been less expensive to continue sending them overseas for their education than to build and maintain their own university, President Nyerere believed it was well worth the extra cost.

The first thing I did when I arrived on the campus was to secure an appointment with the University Principal, intending to ask his expectations of my position. He said he had some very definite things that he expected, but he instead thought it best if he asked me first what were my intentions for the position, since I came with excellent qualifications. I jumped at the opportunity.

My first goal, I said, was to encourage all students to involve themselves wholeheartedly in the University process, since its search for truth, its dissemination of knowledge, and its service to the new nation was itself a godly task. I acknowledged that the University, admittedly 'secular' and 'positively neutral' toward all religion and irreligion, nevertheless should accept the chaplain as an important factor contributing to the attainment of the University's purposes. At this, the Principal began to warm up encouragingly.

Secondly, the chaplain must not become compartmentalized to a 'part' of campus life called the 'religion area', but must actively enter into entire academic, social and cultural life of the University. I would insist on this.

Thirdly, since I represented the Christian Council of Tanganyika, I must faithfully represent all the Protestant bodies within it, so that they feel that the chaplain is their sympathetic and faithful representative, serving their concerns at the University. At the same time, we must genuinely foster the ecumenical spirit on the campus; seeking cooperation with the Catholic chaplain, and with other religious groups as well, especially the Islamic presence there. I could see he was relieved to hear this.

Fourthly, all my efforts would seek to faithfully express and promote the indigenization of Christian theology, ethics, institutions and forms of worship. As an expatriate myself, it was especially important in today's Africa to aid the search for authentic expressions of the African understanding of faith and life. To this end, since it was the University's goal to Africanize as rapidly as possible the administrative and faculty positions, I too was committed to securing a qualified African candidate to succeed me as soon as possible, hopefully in two or three years. Again he was pleased.

Finally, I said, I was a veteran of World War II and had observed many conflicts ending in unproductive violence. Especially knowing of the violence and destruction associated with Africa's quest for Independence all over the continent, especially in Kenya our neighbor to the north, I hoped my experience here would help me better understand how conflicts might be dealt with less violently and with better prospects for constructive and peaceful solutions. Also, I hoped that I might contribute to make that goal a reality for this nation and this University.

"Mr. Principal", I said, "these are my expectations. Do they meet with your approval? And what are your expectations of me?"

He responded after a moment, saying in effect: "I couldn't have said my expectations any better. We're excited to have you here. Count on us to support your efforts here." The following day, at a reception, he met my beautiful and charming wife, after which he told me "I didn't anticipate such charming people for our chaplain – and, especially your wife". Again, I thought as I had on numerous other occasions, it sure helps to have an attractive and charming wife to help open doors in a new venture.

In general, I came to believe that Ecumenical relationships in East Africa were far better than they were in the United States, and that perhaps the missionary efforts in Africa during the past century, which had a bad reputation in the US, weren't so bad after all. I felt that relationships among all religious groups, and between Church and State, were healthier than in the states. The Churches in Tanganyika were now Independent and led by Africans who were making their own decisions. Originally, Christians from overseas had started in that country most formal education, schools, hospitals and medical care. Now, however, I was one of the representatives appointed by the Church to assist in the process of turning over control of these institutions to the new government. At the time, missionary teachers from foreign countries were still considered essential for conducting secondary and higher education, and they would continue until their positions could be Africanized. This had not been true for the several hundred United States Peace Corps teachers who during my three years there would be expelled by the government on charges of destroying African culture and undermining government policies. In general, compared to Western Governments and Businesses, I believe Christian Missionary efforts rated far better in their relationships to the real needs of the people of East Africa.

At the University, the Law School's Extension Division offered short courses for Magistrates, called Judges in America, to help them better serve in the New Africa. These men had received little of the formal education that modern Law Schools would have required. Most had been tribal chiefs or '*mzees*' (meaning wise old men and highly respected in their traditional African world) who had been appointed Magistrates in this new African nation. The regular Law Faculty gave them a short course in the practice of modern law. I was asked to conduct a special series of classes called Human Relations, combining basic insights from modern psychology, sociology and religion and applying them to common problems they might face in their practice. I'm not sure that they learned much from me, however they taught me a great deal about their views and the wisdom of traditional African life.

For example, in one session I asked what they thought about the practice of law as it was taught at the law school and to be applied in East Africa. They began laughing among themselves. Only after much encouragement from me did they finally reveal that conducting court as the Law School advocated just wouldn't work in rural Africa. It might work in the West (Europe or America), but not for them. And further, their opinion was that it wasn't even working well for us in the West. From what they understood, no one left a law court happy in the West, or if one party left happy, the other party left angry. If someone 'won', then someone else had to 'lose'. In such a system, friendships ended in the courtroom, revenge and division resulted among the parties involved, and the community was torn apart. They felt this would be tragic for life in Africa, where the goal of their jobs was to restore community, restore friendship and restore loyalties of those in the tribe or among tribes. The traditional way was to bring together the two sides, get them to talk together until a commonly agreed on reconciling solution was reached. When the chief finally announced a judgment, it was one that restored good relationship and community, not alienation and resentment. One old 'mzee' related that one of his decisions, after hours of discussion by many members of both families and their tribes, had required one family to offer a cow to the other family, to which both had agreed. This was followed by the receiving family butchering the cow for a gigantic all night party celebration with dancing and drumming and drinking 'pombe' provided by both families, families in this case being whole clans of people. Wow, I thought, if only our law practices in the U.S. could achieve these results of reconciliation and community and justice. I was to learn more about these concepts, which they called 'ujamaa'.

Shortly after my arrival in East Africa, Tanganyika and Zanzibar were united to become one nation, to be known as Tanzania, uniting their close historical relationship following their recent colonial past.

Following Independence, one of the first acts of President Nyerere had been to establish the University. Nyerere was a frequent visitor on the campus. I had been privileged to have been introduced to him, and grew to have a deep respect for him. In reading a tribute he had made to Dag Hammarskjoeld, the first Secretary General of the UN, I learned a great deal about Nyerere's own thinking and values. He described his understanding of Hammarskjoeld's purpose for the UN as being chiefly to search for peace in the world, and naturally that caught my attention for my own quest of peacemaking. Hammarskjoeld's way of bringing reconciliation to quarreling parties before their disputes developed into violent conflicts was to get them to talk to one another, and keep talking until agreement was reached. It confirmed my own conviction that agreeing to talk and keep talking is an essential alternative to violence, whether between two persons or two nations. Likewise, Nyerere insisted that since it is man's inalienable right to revolt against laws or conditions that offend basic human rights, as the American Declaration of Independence declared, concern for peace must also be a accompanied by concern creating the necessary conditions for peace, which is justice. He recognized that during the era of nationalism, people had been led toward exclusive national loyalties and concepts of national superiority, which inevitably led to the political point of view that often it was easier to fight than to talk. Therefore, he saw the challenge facing us today to be the conversion of nationalism into internationalism, just as the individual must seek not only his own welfare but the 'common good' as well.

Nyerere also saw the danger of disenchantment from expecting too much from the UN or the new African nations, as well as unrealistic expectations for the easy settlement of disputes by simply talking together. He recognized that Nationalism made nations suspicious of one another and unwilling to surrender national sovereignty to a more desirable international outlook. However, he also recognized that at the same time we are all also moving in the opposite direction toward a 'one world' reality as nations move ever closer to one another, leading to greater conflict possibilities. He urged all leaders to follow Hammarskjoeld's example of courage and patience to keep talking and negotiating, holding to principals of a common humanity, and willingness to think and act beyond allegiance to individual or national loyalties and willingness to sacrifice their own reputation and life for the larger loyalty.

I was surprised to hear Nyerere speak to students at the university as 'servants in training'. He addressed the elite of the nation, these first few hundred students to attend the nation's only University, the leaders of the future, as 'servants'. Many of these students felt themselves entitled to the best, expecting a future at the very top of the social, business and governmental world, but were now being addressed as 'servants in training'. I tried to imagine students at Harvard or Yale being addressed this way. I remembered the many times I had given sermons in church about Jesus' teachings regarding 'servanthood', and calling them to service and ministry to others, especially poor and suffering people. Now here was the president of the nation, speaking to students at a secular University, sounding like a 'preacher'. I was inspired to hear a politician applying Christian ideals to national political goals in a secular University setting.

Nyerere said he expected two things of the University—to be completely objective in the search for truth, but also to be committed to the service of all the people of the nation. In a developing society of rapid social change where the vast majority of the people live in poverty, education must be committed to the people of that nation and their humanistic goals. He constantly reminded all of us that the only justification for creating the University and giving it high priority for their scarce financial resources, especially in this poverty-stricken society, was for it to contribute to transforming the national poverty. Nyerere, a well educated and devout Catholic Christian, appealed to both humanitarian ideals and to their traditional African culture, as expressed by *'Ujamaa'* and *'African Socialism'*.

'African Socialism' emphasized two aspects. The *'Socialism'* part affirmed the communal aspects of their nation's public policy, the common good, and rejected sole reliance on the West's capitalism and individualistic profit driven public policy. The *'African'* part affirmed the traditional African ways of communal life, and rejected the Communist's economic determinism and hierarchical socialistic driven public policy. *'African Socialism'* was their 'third way' of non-alignment with Cold War divisions. This 'third way' proved a most difficult balancing act for the Nyerere government however, as the two superpowers pursued the newly independent nations to choose sides in the Cold War withholding economic aid and trade and threatening destabilization tactics for failure to demonstrate a clear allegiance. In determining to adopt "a policy of non-alignment concerning international conflicts which do not concern us," Nyerere cited the saying: "when the elephants fight it is the grass which gets crushed." Traditional societies emphasized their communal nature where everyone was fully aware of being

part of the tribe, their community, and their togetherness. It was a 'classless society', *'ujamaa'*, all living the same sort of life, a hard and difficult life to be sure, but one co-operatively lived together, interdependent, each sharing responsibility and the rewards of life together. They believed that *'Uhuru'*, their freedom now as an independent nation, must build upon their cultural heritage. The educational policy of students being considered 'servants in training' was to be a natural expression of *'African Socialism'* and *'Ujamaa'*.

Toward the end of 1966 the government issued a new National Service Proposal, which would require all students, including University students, to serve following graduation for eighteen months of service to the nation. For these eighteen months they would retain only 40% of their salary, 60% being repaid to the government. Many Tanzanian students objected to the proposal, claiming it exploited them, and planned to protest at the State House. After reviewing the proposal, I felt that it was good and fair, and proceeded over several evenings to invite groups of students to our home to discuss it. I suggested to them that compared to students in America, their treatment by the government was very generous. They had received all their education free, and had even received free housing and a living allowance during their University years. I mentioned that many American students were serving in the Peace Corps voluntarily following graduation. Further, since half the Tanzanian children had never had the opportunity to even begin to go to school and fewer yet had been able to go to secondary school, let alone the University, the nation was right to require these fortunate University students to take responsibility to help begin correcting this national problem. I told them my Christian values led me to support the call to National Service, though I equally admired and respected their culture of *African Socialism* and *ujamaa* that could now be more fully realized in their *uhuru*. Unfortunately, many did not agree with me, and reminded me that as an expatriate in their country I was to refrain from interfering with their political policies.

Finally, on the morning of October 22, nearly 400 students, over 300 of them from the University, marched in mass to the State

House, and read their ultimatum to the President. They objected to the terms proposed for their National Service, described the exploitation they felt they would suffer under the Proposal, and said that "our bodies could be forced into National Service, but not our spirits." Further, they insisted that the battle between the political elite and educated elite would be perpetually continued.

No sooner had the ultimatum been read than the President responded. He told them National Service was consistent with the African way of life, and that everyone in the nation had their part to play in the national effort. He agreed that salaries in Government were too high, that there must not be a political elite. Turning to the Finance Minister, he told him that he wanted his own salary cut 20% immediately and permanently. Further, he said, that all high Government salaries were to be cut, because all high salaried people and these students were in the same favored class, supported by those on minimal wages and the poor peasants. The President then told the students that he understood their ultimatum that "they would not cooperate in spirit." Therefore, he said he would not force anyone to join the National Service, but that he would not accept anyone whose spirit was not in it. Therefore, he told them, their education for now was ended and they were going home, where, in the presence of their parents and fellow tribesmen, they would learn again of true African ways, of the common good, of *ujamaa*, and what *uhuru* meant to the country, and to be "servants in training." They were immediately surrounded by police, fingerprinted at the police station, loaded onto trucks, returned to the University to collect their belongings, and trucked back to the homes of their parents. The next day we learned that 394 students had been sent home, over 300 of them from the University.

Everyone remaining at the University, administration, faculty and remaining students, immediately began a review of how education in the nation, and especially in higher education, could better constructively serve the task of transforming the lives of their poverty stricken people. Not only we expatriates, but also the Tanzanians and other Africans, had experienced the models of education which prevailed in the more developed nations in North America, Europe and the USSR, and then had introduced those models into Africa during the colonial period. This tended to produce students with elitist social attitudes, which did not serve the needs of this poor country. I had observed this especially while traveling in Uganda and Kenya, where some students paraded around with a cane and dressed like English Gentlemen, the model they had learned through the educational process. All too often, students were tempted to regard themselves as a group who had rights without responsibilities. It was to this task of producing *'servants-in-training'* that we committed ourselves.

It was only later after returning to the United States that I realized that this concept of 'servants-in-training', while appropriate in an African context, was inappropriate in an American context, especially for blacks. James Cone, the black theologian, clearly demonstrated this. White society, even among active church folk and especially in the south, while they may not rape or lynch African Americans, still lived in and enjoyed a society that expected blacks to be white people's servants, to plow their fields, clean their houses, and mow their lawns, as well as worship in separate churches or sit in the white church balconies and attend segregated schools and drink from 'colored only' drinking fountains. From this experience in America, black people needed to reject the idea of 'servanthood'. Whites usually called this view 'black racism', but blacks called the prevailing policy 'white racism.' And in this American context, I agreed. Only after our society becomes free from the evil of racism, will the concept of 'servanthood' become a powerful and ethical expression of community, of ujamaa, of the common good, of Dr. King's Beloved Community.

We expatriates had been part of the problem. We had come from different cultures, with different life styles and with standards of living far different from what prevailed in East Africa. Most of us at the University were well aware of this and tried diligently to live adapted to African ways. This was difficult even for well-educated and urbanized Africans, but was nearly impossible for expatriates. I had observed this problem even among the American Peace Corps volunteers who were serving in the country, who probably lived in conditions as 'close to the earth' as possible, yet stuck out like a sore thumb in the villages in which they served. Once when discussing this with a group of Peace Corps volunteers, one of them, Rodney, a black American volunteer, said that it was no easier for him than for the white volunteers, that Tanzanians considered him a Western American and not a Black American. I was not surprised that during my time there, the Peace Corps was expelled from Tanzania. It was rumored that the reason for this was that a few of them were actually spies reporting to the CIA. However, the real reason seemed to be that having Westerners living in their villages and teaching in their schools, even under the best conditions of identifying with African life, was disruptive and undermining their African Culture as the nation attempted to build a New African Society, or African Socialism.

The University at Dar es Salaam made considerable progress toward creating a more African-friendly environment during my last six months there. Likewise, almost all the expelled students a year later were able to return after experiencing life again in their home communities, hopefully better prepared for their education toward being servants-in-training.

My three years in East Africa had passed quickly. I left with a warm heart toward the people of Tanzania. They, along with the rest of Africa, were facing the tremendous challenge of having been thrust suddenly into the post-colonial era of national independence and a rapidly changing world. Much of what Europe and the United States had faced over several centuries was now confronting them in mere generations. While their domestic obstacles were many, they always faced the impact of neo-colonial pressures, East-West world rivalries and Cold War interests. However, my family and I had only experienced friendly and positive personal relationships. They had given me as much or more than I had given them, and it was with a profound gratitude that I was able to turn over my position as Protestant Chaplain to Dr. Omari, a well educated and capable Tanzanian, and say goodbye to many good friends, and head for San Francisco after three years abroad.

As my family and I left Africa and traveled home in 1967 I was fortunate to have been invited to Prague, Czechoslovakia, for a meeting with the Executive Committee of the World Student Christian Federation (WSCF) to report to them about my experience in East Africa. I had previously arranged to purchase a Volkswagen squareback in Germany and then for our family to camp for several weeks throughout Europe before going to Vienna, Austria, to attend a Lutheran World Federation biannual conference. It was a rare occasion for the WSCF to meet in a Communist country, and I was thrilled at the invitation. We had the opportunity to meet with faculty and students of Prague's famous Charles University as well as from a Protestant seminary. Although our discussions with them in the arranged meetings were interesting, it was our long off the record conversations afterwards when we would talk into the wee hours of the morning, over a few steins of beer, that were really rewarding. I was surprised by their criticism of communism, their openness to Western ideas, and their demands for radical reform in their society. It was the first time I heard the names of writers and poets and intellectuals like Vaclav Havel (later to become President of the democratic Czech Republic) and Alexander Dubcek who were demanding the abolition of censorship and the secret police, greater parliamentary rights and no restrictions on religious freedom.

What I observed was all part of a cultural reawakening that contributed within a few months to the political reform movement led by Dubcek known as the Prague Spring. Dubcek, who succeeded Antonin Novotny as First Secretary, was advocating such things as the dismantling of the agricultural collectives into small private farms with the farmers actually owning the land and being able to sell their produce, and to the democratization of trade unions, the courts, and local governments. I had actually seen the beginnings of 'socialism with a human face', a middle way between communism and capitalism, that called for freedom of speech, press, assembly and religious observances and introduction of some private enterprise. At the same time a Christian resurgence was happening, and serious efforts were being made to engage in dialog between Marxists and Christian Theologians.

I was not surprised later that by August 1968, in retaliation, Soviet troops invaded the country ending the reform movement. However, after seeing the vitality and energy that led up to that reform, neither was I surprised that twenty years later massive nonviolent demonstrations led to the downfall of Czechoslovakia's Communist regime.

Leaving Czechoslovakia, we traveled by car to Berlin, going through Communist East Germany, and had a rewarding experience on the way. We had difficulty at the border crossing getting permission to enter Soviet controlled East Germany. After much negotiation, we were given a permit allowing us one day to pass through East Germany on the autobahn to Berlin. An hour later we were nearly out of gas and still had a long distance to go, so I turned off toward a village I could see not far away. However, it was Sunday, and no petrol station was open. A sign pointed to another town about fifteen kilometers away, and we headed there. There were no petrol stations on the way, nor as I entered the town. Suddenly, the engine stopped. I was out of gas. I didn't know what to do.

About that time, a uniformed Army Officer happened to be walking by on a Sunday afternoon stroll, accompanied by his wife and a young lad. He said something to me, which in my poor knowledge of German I took to be something like "Do you have a problem?" I answered in my poor German "Ich nine petrol" and then asked "donde esta Petrol station?" forgetting that what I said was in my poor Spanish, not German. He was a little confused by my question, but seemed to understand, and managed to convey to me that he had petrol at his house, and for me to follow walking with him home. We walked along for a couple blocks, his boy and mine seeming to have a grand time chasing each other. The Officer pulled out a cigarette, and offered me one. Although I don't smoke, I appreciated his offer and friendliness, and accepted. As he struck a match, and lit my cigarette, I noticed how odd the cigarette was, like none I had ever seen. It was half filter, and had some strange letters in writing on it. About this time he asked as he pointed to me, "English?' and I said "no, American." and then I asked pointing to him "German?" and he said "nein, Russian." In a flash it dawned on me that here was one of those Communists who we were in a Cold War with, and his look suggested that it had just dawned on him also. I almost threw up my arms in a self-defensive posture, and suspected that he might have done so too. Fortunately the reaction quickly passed, as we both broke into laughter and continued on to his home. There, we got into his car, drove to the other side of the village to a petrol station. Although it was closed, it had a dozen five gallon gas cans under lock, and with his key he unlocked one can which we took back to my stalled car and poured the gas into the tank. I tried to pay him for the gas, and he refused to accept it, gave me a big smile, gave directions to the autobahn, and sent us on our way.

I had never liked the way we were conducting the Cold War, believing it a negative and unproductive way to deal with our relationship with the Soviets. After this chance meeting with one of the 'enemy's' soldiers, I was more convinced than ever that there must be a better way.

Shortly thereafter I had another similar experience. Spending a few days in West Berlin, we decided to venture into East Berlin for a day. After passing through *Checkpoint Charley* border crossing, and touring the Soviet occupied area, we chanced upon a large Memorial Park, built by the Soviets to honor their soldiers killed in WWII. It contained many monuments with quotations from Lenin, Stalin, and other Soviet heroes. Apparently it also was a site where they brought truckloads of their present army personnel for outing and recreation. There were hundreds of young soldiers in uniform walking around, laughing and having a good time. Most of them looked as if they were in their late teens or early twenties, both tall and short, with red or blond or dark hair, some with Asian features and others a variety of Caucasian features – in other words, they looked and acted like they could have been a group of American soldiers out on liberty. Twenty of them were standing in one place, and after first asking my wife, Dru, I asked the group's permission to take a picture of her standing among them. She stood in the middle of the bunch as I stepped back and took a Polaroid camera picture of her and the group. After a minute or so the picture developed, and I was pleased and smiled as I showed it to her. They were curious, and approached us to see the picture. I suspect they had never seen Polaroid before. Then one of them, using sign language, asked if he could have a picture taken with her. Unfortunately I had used my last film and was unable to take another picture. The memory I retain is of an army of Soviet soldiers, fun loving and laughing and appreciating a beautiful woman, in the same way any group of Americans would. I was further convinced that many political leaders, people with wealth, people with business interests, munitions makers and others in both countries may profit from the Cold War, but that the 'people' of both lands had more in common with each other than with their own war oriented leaders.

"We are only just beginning to understand the power of love and nonviolence because we are just beginning to understand the weakness of force and oppression."

—*Cesar Chavez*

CAMPUS PASTOR PEDERSEN MOMENTS BEFORE HIS ARREST DURING DEMONSTRATION
AT SAN FRANCISCO STATE UNIVERSITY

CAMPUS PASTOR PEDERSEN SHORTLY
AFTER HIS ARREST DURING
DEMONSTRATION AT SAN FRANCISCO
STATE UNIVERSITY

OUCH!!!!!!
IT HURTS

PHOTOS COURTESY OF AP/WIDE WORLD PHOTOS

Chapter 6

1967-70: The Storm Comes

UPON REACHING THE STATES in the summer of 1967, I experienced a cultural shock as great as the shock I had experienced upon my arrival in the different culture of Africa. At least I had expected the African culture shock. To my surprise, however, upon arriving in America it seemed to me to be a militarized society. In New York I saw policemen wearing black leather jackets setting in their large police cars with rifles mounted in the front seats. In Africa we seldom saw uniformed policemen, and in London the British police carried no guns and drove little white and green cars similar to a VW Bug. Even more to my surprise was the majority support for the Vietnam War and their anger at students protesting against it. When I left the States in 1964, Goldwater had been considered the Hawk, urging stronger military action in Vietnam, while Johnson had been the dove, urging restraint. Shortly after I had left the States, Johnson had been overwhelmingly reelected, and Goldwater repudiated. Now, three years later, Johnson was defending his ever-expanding promotion of the war.

I was eager to get back to the United States and to Herb Caen's 'City-by-the-Bay', not only because San Francisco is an exciting city, but even more because I was to become Campus Minister at San Francisco State University. I had turned down other attractive offers, and had selected SFSU because it had several special things going for it. Among them were a special entry and study program for Black Students, an Experimental College that offered some truly creative options, some Curriculum Reform projects by students and faculty in the area of Teacher Training, and a strong Ecumenical Campus Ministry deeply involved in the University's entire life.

During my first summer back in America we saw flower children overrunning San Francisco, Arlo Guthrie saying "you can't trust anyone over thirty", and the young not trusting any of the authorities. It was 1967, 'the summer of love', with Jimmy Hendricks busting his guitar at a concert as a cultural expression, the 'pill' enabling the sexual revolution, and increasing experimentation with drugs.

When I arrived on the campus in San Francisco, most of its students and faculty were decidedly against the war. I soon got filled in on the three years I had been gone. About the time I was leaving the States in 1964, the supposed attack on an American destroyer in the Gulf of Tonkin resulted in giving President Johnson almost unlimited power to take stronger unlimited military action in Vietnam. Although the incident turned out to be a fake, and that responsible American officials had lied about it, over two hundred thousand troops were sent there the following year, and a half million by 1968.

On the positive side, while I had been in Africa, President Johnson had pushed through his Civil Rights Acts and the War on Poverty, seeking in his way to eliminate these vestiges of injustice. M.L. King had continued to use nonviolent direct action seeking to fulfill his hope and dream of equality for all Americans. However, after the Watts riots in Los Angeles in 1965 and in Newark and Detroit in 1967 M.L. King began to express his "disappointment in America". He said "You can't talk about solving the economic problem of the Negro without talking about billions of dollars. You can't talk about ending the slums without first saying profit must be taken out of slums. We are saying that something is wrong... there must be a better distribution of wealth and maybe America must move toward a democratic socialism." He called for a revolution of values regarding poverty and wealth. On the campus of San Francisco State, most students and faculty enthusiastically responded to King's message, especially those in SDS (Students for a Democratic Society) and the Black Student Union.

During my first summer back in the U.S. in 1967, the National Advisory Commission on Civil Disorders had been commissioned by President Johnson to investigate the urban riots in the black sections of Los Angeles (1965), Chicago (1966), and Newark (1967) and other major cities. Its task was to analyze the specific causes resulting in the riots, the deeper causes of the worsening racial climate, and potential remedies to resolve them.

Its report, called The Kerner Report, was released in 1968, and concluded that the causes of urban riots was the profound frustration of inner-city blacks from the racism deeply embedded in American society. It warned that the United States was "moving toward two societies, one black, one white—separate and unequal." The problems that fell particularly on African Americans were not only overt discrimination, but also chronic poverty, high unemployment, inadequate housing, lack of access to health care, poor schools, and police bias and brutality. It recommended specific actions to improve conditions. With the growing unrest on our campus, I was heartened by the report and recommendations, convinced as I was that an honest awareness of the problem, and understanding its causes, was the first step in its resolution. Unfortunately the implementation of the recommendations was later largely ignored, especially after the election of Nixon at the end of the year.

In early 1968, King led the effort to organize the Poor People's Campaign to address issues of economic justice. It was to end with a March on Washington, D.C. demanding Congress end its 'hostility to the poor' by enacting a Poor People's Bill of Rights calling for a massive government jobs program in America's cities, and a radical reconstruction of society by correcting the serious flaws of racism, poverty and militarism. After months of traveling the country organizing people for the Campaign, but before the March on Washington had been completed, King was assassinated on April 4th.

In the 1960s there had been many ways to be part of the civil rights movement. M.L. King, Jr. used peaceful, nonviolent methods, while the Black Panthers and Bobby Seale and Huey Newton were willing to use violence if necessary against violent repression.

Medgar Evers worked through the NAACP using legal and political methods. Malcolm X and Elijah Muhammad and the Nation of Islam chose the emphasis on Black self-affirmation and independence. Muhammad Ali joined the Nation of Islam to promote Black pride and equality. All of these had the goal of leading to a change of consciousness, from 'Negro' to 'Black' to 'African-American', and to Black Pride, freedom, justice and equality for Black people in America.

The development of Muhammad Ali at this time was interesting to watch. By 1967 Muhammad Ali, the former Cassius Clay, and the reigning heavyweight champion of the world, faced a momentous decision. When he was reclassified 1-A and eligible for induction for duty in Vietnam, he knew he could continue his boxing career and remain heavyweight champion if he registered for the draft and faced induction. But he honestly felt this violated his religious beliefs and therefore declared himself a conscientious objector. He didn't agree with our war in Vietnam, and even more he felt he couldn't kill people he had never known or had never done him or his country any harm. He was not a draft dodger, nor did he run to Canada, nor did he hide in his own country. Instead, he refused to be inducted into the military, knowing that everything he had worked for during his lifetime was on the line and knowing that he faced prison when he refused induction. Even though he was stripped of his championship title, his passport taken from him so that he couldn't fight overseas, his prime boxing years denied him, and even though his Nation of Islam expelled him and refused to allow association with him, he never regretted his decision.

This decision had been a long time in the making. It had really begun in 1960, when he, then known as Cassius Clay, became Olympic Champion upon winning the Olympic Gold Metal in Rome. Later that summer, returning to his home in Louisville, Kentucky, he was given the 'Key to the City' by its Mayor. Later, he and his friend went into a little restaurant to order cheeseburgers, although he knew that in the past Negroes would not have been served there. Surely, he felt, now it was different. Sitting there proud with his gold medal around his neck, he was told by the waitress that: "We don't serve Negroes here." With pride, he told her he was

Cassius Clay, the Olympic Champion, pointing to his gold medal, saying, "I won the Gold Medal for America." After conferring with the manager, the waitress came back and told him, "Sorry, but you will have to leave." When he went out, Cassius later wrote:

> "What had it meant when the mayor gave him the 'Key to the City'? What did it mean that you could earn a Gold Medal for your country but couldn't eat in a restaurant in your own home-town where you had been born and gone to school, because of the color of your skin? And even if it could have gotten him into a 'White Only' place, what did it mean if other Black people were excluded? He began realizing that if his Gold Medal didn't mean equality for ALL, it didn't mean anything at all."

That day he stopped wearing his Gold Medal around his neck.

Now, seven years later in 1967, Ali followed his conscience and deepest convictions, and refused to serve in the military, regardless of the penalties he would have to pay. His conscience was clear, and he said he "never felt so free".

About this time, we at Ecumenical House interpreted 'ecumenism' to be broader than being limited only to Protestants. In this spirit we campus ministers sent a letter to Muhammad Ali inviting him to be the Minister, or 'Iman', representing Islam, and ministering to Muslims on the campus. Although he thanked us profusely for this, and for supporting his act of conscience, he said he regretfully had to decline. In the same spirit, around this time, the Catholic Newman Chaplain, and later a Jewish Rabbi, became part of our ecumenical ministry as well.

Vietnam was increasingly commanding my attention, as it did the entire nation. Protests increased against the Draft, especially with college-aged young people, leading to Draft resistance and Draft Card burning. Earlier, one of our campus ministers agreed to be a supervisor for COs (Conscientious Objectors) and the Draft Board assigned us over twenty-eight COs to supervise. Most of these were the finest of our American young men, idealistic, spiritually sensitive, and with high personal values. However, a few were of questionable mental stability, and a few others were into drugs. The Draft Boards were anxious to keep these few out of the service, and gladly assigned them to us. When the supervising campus minister was later transferred to a different campus, I inherited the supervision task, for which I felt unprepared. I came to highly respect most of the COs and felt it a privilege to support them doing outstanding volunteer community service as an expression of their faith, though was concerned that the Feds would somehow hold me responsible for the few who were mentally unstable or into drugs. However, we were never challenged in our supervision, and were even thanked for it.

By the summer of 1968 it was clearly evident on our campus that the storm of protest and change was reaching its peak. The earlier assassination of President Kennedy in 1963 had been followed by the assassination of the American Black Muslim leader Malcolm X in 1965. By 1967 M.L. King had connected his attack on racism and poverty to militarism and the Vietnam War, publicly declaring: "America was the greatest conveyer of violence in the world." Then during the first half of 1968 we experienced the assassination of M.L. King on April 4 and Bobby Kennedy two months later on June 6th. The race turmoil in Watts (either riots or insurrection, depending on your point-of-view) and the protests at the Chicago democratic presidential nominating convention during the summer, were clearly signs of frustration with the continuing racism in American society and anger at further escalation of the war in Vietnam.

Following the assassination of King, students, not only black students, but also whites, swarmed around our ministry center. They had identified with his "I have a dream" message, with his call for a true revolution of values, for fundamental changes in the political and economic life of the nation, with his opposition to the war, and his desire to see a redistribution of resources to correct racial and economic injustice. One student quoted from King's "I've been to the Mountain top" speech made the night before he was assassinated:

> "It really doesn't matter now... the talk about threats on my life... what would happen to me from some of our sick white brothers... I just want to do God's will.

He's allowed me to go up to the mountaintop! And I've looked over, and I've seen the Promised Land. I may not get there with you. But I want you to know that we, as a people, will get to the Promised Land. I'm not worried about anything. I'll not fear any man. My eyes have seen the Glory of the coming of the Lord."

It was clear that these students and faculty had been inspired by King's 'Dream', and deeply hurt and disillusioned by his death. When we asked them to pray (and we did pray with them) that this 'Dream' soon be realized, and to act (and we did urge them to act) to begin making this 'Dream' come true, we had no doubt they were determined to make it happen.

Two months following King's assassination, Bobby Kennedy was assassinated. Again on our campus we experienced the same kind of scene that had taken place after King's assassination. However, I saw an interesting difference in the journeys each man had taken leading to his death. King had begun life in the midst of the discrimination and suffering of the black community, developed a deeply religious and spiritual faith leading to the Christian ministry, and then his experience led him to express this faith in Direct Nonviolence Action with all its social and political implications. Bobby Kennedy, on the other hand, had grown up amid affluence and all the benefits of the white community, and then followed his father's urgings and his brother John's example to enter into a political career. It was only later that his experiences led him to express more profound and idealistic humanitarian goals in his political life. Fortunately, he was able to draw upon his Catholic religious and spiritual background. During the 1950s, Bobby Kennedy had been identified with the McCarthy anti-communist witch-hunts and with opposition to the Teamster's Labor Union, and in general showed little support for justice and peace efforts. However, as Attorney General in the 60s, many were surprised to find him moving aggressively to enforce Civil Rights in the South on race issues.

Finally, only months before his death, he took the courageous step of supporting Cesar Chavez's farm workers movement. Early in 1968 I was able to go with some students to Delano to be supportive of Chavez and the United Farm Workers in their grape strike. This was the first but not the last time I was to see and support Chavez, and the only time I would see Bobby Kennedy, who joined the strikers that day out in the fields where he shared the bread and wine of Holy Communion with the strikers. Kennedy linked his call for the end of the Vietnamese War to the poverty and racism in America and the grape strike. But I was even more impressed with Chavez's insistence that the strike be conducted nonviolently. That day I heard him remind them:

> "You've been trained for this struggle. You've been kicked and beaten and attacked by dogs and jailed, but you've been taught not to quit or flee in shame, but to resist, not with retaliation but to overcome with love, with hard work, with dignity and persistence, and nonviolently ...and with prayer and fasting and following the way of Jesus."

It was about this time that President Johnson made the surprise announcement that he would not run again for president in the coming elections. Only then did Bobby Kennedy declare a week later on March 12th his entry into the Presidential race. Many believe that only the splitting of the anti-war vote between Bobby Kennedy and Eugene McCarthy, even though Bobby had been assassinated before the election, allowed Hubert Humphrey to become the democratic nominee, resulting in Richard Nixon finally becoming president, and the resulting escalation of the Vietnamese war.

Only with this as the background could one understand what would soon take place on the campus at San Francisco State University as the new term began in 1968: massive student and faculty protests and a strike, the longest and one of the most violent campus conflicts in our nations history. This included the firing of the SFSU president and the installation, over the faculty senate's objection, of the new president S.I. Hayakawa, who vowed to use 'all necessary force to keep the campus open' (echoing the Vietnam War words 'we had to destroy the village in order to save it'). And for me, it meant being arrested, Hayakawa demanding I be removed from my ministry, and my Bishop refusing to do so, and instead supporting my continuing ministry there as being faithful to the purposes for which the church had asked me to be there.

Getting ready for the opening of the new college year, I had celebrated some very happy personal experiences. During the summer my wife and I celebrated twenty years of a happy marriage, together with our high school son, Brad, and jr. high school daughter, Kim. Then, a few weeks later my wife gave me the gift of our second son, Scott, which seemed to me a sign that in the midst of profound conflict, new life is always emerging. Within a month the strike started at my campus, and a month later, my friend and colleague Father Peter Sammon, also in campus ministry, came to report to my wife that a half hour earlier I had been arrested on the campus and taken to jail. New life and continuing conflict seems the reality in life.

The decade of the 60s was a time of change, and although many saw only negative developments, others, including myself, saw them as positive and necessary for America to attain a more mature democracy. Even as the civil rights movement—the sit ins, protest marches, Martin Luther King's nonviolent direct actions, legislation for racial equality—were important positive acts bringing about constructive change to unjust situations, so also was the purpose of the SFSU Strike seen as an effort to achieve and maintain the constructive academic life of that university, especially changes called for in the Kerner Report earlier that year. The Strike could only be understood knowing the anger and rejection of youth and students toward the Vietnam War, especially those facing a military draft for a war they didn't believe in. Also the assassination of John F. Kennedy five years earlier, and then the assassinations of Martin Luther King, Jr., and Robert Kennedy a few months earlier in 1968, each of whom students saw as persons of hope for fulfillment of their dreams for America, confirmed for them that America would only develop positively if they had the courage to act to change the injustices in our civil life, including the administration of our campus. Likewise, the largely white SDS (Students for a Democratic Society) movement throughout the USA, the violence of the police during the protests at the Chicago Democratic Presidential Convention immediately before the opening of the fall term in 68, the popular grape strike of Cesar Chavez's National Farm Workers so near to our campus in California, were all precursors of the strike that followed at the SFSU campus.

After serving at other universities in the States and in East Africa, I had eagerly accepted the invitation to serve at SFSU beginning in the fall of 1967, not only for the opportunity of sharing the gospel's good news of the love and acceptance of God and the power of forgiveness and reconciliation and for seeking the always begging fulfillment of the dream of a new age in human relationships, but especially because of its reputation as an exciting campus, a pioneer of promising innovations in urban-oriented college education. In many ways the college was itself a reflection of "the city." An Experimental College program had emerged which largely abandoned the typical lecture method of teaching. A Community Involvement Program was initiated by students, and supported by the college, in response to the plight of the city and an understanding of the purpose of a college. A Black Studies Program had developed over several years, by this time containing twenty-two courses taught in different departments of the college. When I arrived in 1967 I found a liberal president and administration, faculty, and students generally committed to the furtherance of all these programs and goals.

By the beginning of the 1968 academic year all of these programs, many of these the very reason I had chosen to come to this campus a year before, were under serious threat. Withdrawal of funds, restrictions on programs and campus politics and some minority faculty led to growing dissatisfaction with administration and faculty. Student government had come to represent the more aggressive community action groups more than the indifferent general student body. This led to the call of a student strike beginning November 6 by the Black Students Union and the Third World Liberation Front. The strike brought the underlying disorders of the larger society to a head on our campus, which focused on the chronic blocking of the aspirations of minority students. Their growing commitment to direct action, as a means of forcing change quickly, ran afoul of the governance system of the State College Board of Trustees and the legislature and governor, who moved at their own bureaucratic pace and cumbersome decision making processes.

While the strike had the support of most white students and many of the faculty, the initiative and leadership for the strike was taken by minority students, especially black students, who were deeply dissatisfied with the college's efforts to meet their needs. The exciting campus conditions that had been developing for several years prior to my coming began to change, especially the conditions that were the reasons for my choosing to come as campus pastor at SFSU in 1967. Restrictions and withdrawal of funds from off-campus community programs and campus politics and some minority faculty led to growing dissatisfaction with the administration and faculty. Students saw them as practicing on campus the same typical white power resistance in correcting the imbalances in economic and social structures, especially those that divided people-of-color from the dominant population.

President Johnson's 'Commission on Civil Disorders' had earlier said that the nation was heading toward two societies, one black and the other white, separate and unequal. I remember Nesbit, one of the black student leaders, saying to me outside Ecumenical House: "Heading toward! Hell NO! These divisions already exist, have existed since the days of slavery, and are now being perpetuated on this campus." While the concept of 'Student Power' was being used at SFSU as it was on most campuses at this time in America to describe the movement of students to demand a share in university policies, on this campus black students added 'Black Power' to describe their efforts to resolve these divisions.

Shortly after the strike began, our campus ministry invited all clergy in the area to attend a Clergy Information Session to try to identify the issues which had to be resolved if reconciliation and progress was to be achieved. One hundred twenty clergy came in response to the following statement:

> "The strike, violence on campus, and closing of the school have produced an emotional atmosphere in which it is difficult for both students and the community at large to be aware of some of the key issues. Campus ministry wishes to focus attention on certain basic

issues that are vital to our school, our community, and society in general."

Campus Ministry called attention to three main issues at our campus. First: "The need for educational opportunities, for black and minority students. For example, in the last four years, black student enrollment at the college had dropped from 10% to 4% of the student body, as has other minority numbers. Changed admissions policy and special curricular are urgently needed." Second: "Despite the rapidity of social changes today, universities are increasingly ignored or attacked when they attempt to contribute to the constructive accommodation of change." And third: "If a free institution is to survive, it must be allowed to govern its own internal affairs. Arbitrary intervention by the Board of Trustees or political forces will stifle independent thought and action, seriously weakening the institution."

A few days following this Clergy Information Session trying to understand the issues involved on this campus, president Robert Smith and the administration called for a Campus Convocation, with striking students, faculty, and the administration discussing the college's problems. Although not finally successful, it was Smith's attempt to bring all sides together to wrestle with the issues in hopes of finally peacefully making progress. I was able to attend both days of the convocation, attended by a packed full auditorium and amplified throughout the campus. The leaders of the strike initially used the occasion to blow off a lot of steam, disrespectful of the administrators taking part, and even of faculty, even though many of them were supportive of the students. However, the students were able to firmly state their reasons for the strike and made serious proposals for correcting abuses in the educational process. It is my estimation that more honest education dealing with complaints of minority students, and students in general, had taken place during those two days than in many hundreds of days I have spent on college campus. Sadly, this effort was not to continue.

During this Campus Convocation to discuss the issues over which the strike had been called, our university president, Robert Smith, was summoned to a Trustee's meeting in Southern California, and was severely restricted as to how his administration could deal with campus problems. Rather than submit to this outside interference he resigned – in effect, he was fired. Without following standard customary university procedure of consultation with the faculty senate on appointments, Smith was immediately replaced by Hayakawa as the new president, who agreed to all the Trustee's demands, pledging to "Use all necessary force to keep the campus open"

I remembered my experience back in 1964 while I had been a campus pastor at Portland State University. I had heard Dr. King's speak on our campus, and I had the opportunity afterwards, together with a small group of interested people, to meet for a short time with him. I had the opportunity to express my appreciation for his address and all his previous leadership and actions toward justice. I will never forget the thrust of his words as Dr. King looked at each of us, including me, saying: "I'm tired of people standing on the sidelines mouthing pious irrelevancies while living a life adjusted to the status quo. Especially you pastors, of all people, should know that Jesus disturbed the peace. He was an extremist. Don't be one of those luke-warm Christians. Get off the sidelines. Be an extremist – an extremist for love, not for hate. You're either an extremist for the cause of justice, or an extremist for the preservation of injustice." I went home and read again his 'Letter from the Birmingham Jail.'

Dr. King's words addressed to us that day four years earlier had made a deep impression on me. I didn't feel they were words of judgment, but rather an appeal to my heart and mind, a call to rise up and act. It was a 'ah-ha' existential experience, a kind of conversion experience, a born-again experience, a 'wake up and live, stop talking and start acting, listen to your heart and respond with your hands and feet' call to get serious about my Journey of Peace Making. His words had earlier led me to a ministry in Africa for three years at the University of East Africa in Tanzania. Now they had led me here to this campus in San Francisco, determined not to be 'adjusted to the status quo, but to be an extremist for justice, and not an extremist for the preservation of injustice'. That determination was soon to be severely tested

The first act of the acting president, Hayakawa, was to close the campus over an extended Thanksgiving holiday, and to reopen it Dec. 2. Although having been a campus pastor there for eighteen months, I had never seen or heard him up to this time. I had read some of his statements given a few days earlier, words like "at the heart of the Black Student Union...is a gang of goons, gangsters, con-men, neo-Nazis and common thieves". Knowing that, as a professor of the English language, his choice of words was no accident, chosen to purposely create a view totally destroying the credibility of the student protests and strike, I feared for what would happen when the campus was reopened.

On Dec. 2, Monday morning, while having breakfast at home and listening to the news on TV, I listened to him repeating the same inflaming views about students, especially blacks, and demanding the student strike be canceled, demanding zero tolerance of any strike activity and declaring a state of emergency regulations on campus. Hayakawa's permission would be required for any activity on the campus, including using the traditional 'free speech platform' in the center of the campus. At that point I determined to get down to our campus ministry center, Ecumenical House, immediately. In my office, looking out the window to the campus across the street, I noticed the same Volkswagen Bug that had parked there throughout the strike, with loudspeakers on its roof, announcing, 'The strike is still on. Support the strike'. Very soon I saw a group of about thirty people marching from the Administration Building heading toward the Volkswagen. Sensing trouble, I ran out of my office, crossed the street, and noticed a man who had climbed onto the Volkswagen and begin pulling wires from the loudspeakers. Wanting to stop any acts leading to violence, I stepped on the front bumper and was about to climb atop the Volkswagen and grab the man to stop his actions, when I noticed it was none other than the college president, Hayakawa, who I had been watching on TV an hour earlier. Surprised and confused, I stepped back, only to see him proudly waving the wires in the air as the cameramen got their pictures of him standing up there wearing his colorful tam-o-shanter, which was to become a symbol for the new president who wouldn't stand for any opposition.

I have often wondered what would have happened had I succeeded in stopping his act of disrupting the loudspeaker, with the picture of him in his tam-o-shanter appearing in nearly every newspaper in the country, and instead one of me grabbing his arms tightly and forcing him down from the car. Perhaps an entirely different direction of the campus conflict would have been taken, the later violence avoided, and negotiations instead of domination resulting. More likely, however, I would have been arrested on the spot, made to appear as the violent one, and contributing even more to his popularity by the general public. As it was, his control and manipulation of the media determined later how nearly everything that happened was to be interpreted and understood. And this meant, unfortunately, that the status quo on this campus would be continued, or even worse, that much of what had made this such an attractive campus in the years before in the 1960s would be repealed, rejecting progress toward a more just and vital university campus.

During that week our campus looked like a war zone, with up to 600 police, some mounted on horses, others flying overhead in helicopters, many wearing riot gear and all too often clubbing anyone standing around. On Thursday, Dec. 5, as a 'campus minister' wanting to fulfill my ministry at that campus, I tried to help avoid further conflict escalation by supporting respected student and community leaders in leading the crowd to the free speech platform, where we hoped that we could then get their attention so as to disperse from the campus as ordered by the police. Unfortunately, just before reaching the platform, a line of police quickly formed a barrier cutting off our approach. I don't believe they realized they were making it impossible to get an aroused crowd peacefully off the campus. A black community leader, Dr. Goodlett, a physician, publisher of the primary black newspaper, and vice president of the San Francisco Council of Churches, spoke for all of us, trying to explain our efforts. Turning around to leave was impossible with the hundreds (perhaps thousands) crowded behind us. The police, over a bullhorn, announced we would be arrested unless we turned and left. Dr. Goodlett said we would not resist. I, standing beside him, held out my crossed hands, and said to the helmeted police officer immediately in front of me, "arrest me, I will not resist". At that point, he punched me in the stomach with the end of his billy club, bending me over holding my stomach. Then I felt a blow to my chin and was knocked to the ground. Only later, viewing police recorded films taken that day, did I see the officer to his left swing an uppercut to my face, which had floored me. A picture appeared in most newspapers the next day throughout the country. It showed me wearing my clerical collar and peace symbol cross, with a helmeted policeman in riot gear holding me with a Billy club around my neck, and me with the other hand pointing and protesting to stop another policeman clubbing a student on the head. It was headlined "Campus Minister Jerry Pedersen arrested at SF State College." Later, several dozen different newspapers with this picture were mailed to me from cities throughout the U.S.A., and from friends in Dar es Salaam, Tanzania, Nairobi, Kenya, and the International Copy from Berlin of the Herald Express. I was then put in a paddy wagon and jailed, along with several students and three other community leaders, Dr. Goodlett, a local Methodist minister, and a leader of the Urban League, the four of us later standing trial together.

Fourteen months later the trial was finally ready to begin, which was expected to last at least four to six weeks. During three weeks of Jury Selection, the prosecution made clear they would call to witness S.F. State President S.I. Hayakawa and 26 police officers. My attorney indicated the defense would call to witness Bishop Carl Segerhammer of the six state Pacific Southwest Synod of the Lutheran Church in America, who would testify that he, and the Executive Board of the Synod, after carefully reviewing my activity as Campus Pastor, fully supported the ministry I had been conducting in that capacity at SFSU as faithfully fulfilling what they expected of me. We also would call to witness the Chairman of the Board of United Ministries of Higher Education responsible for Ecumenical House, and a long list of students and faculty who supported my ministry. My attorney was prepared to ask potential jurors "Would you have any objection to a minister of God being where the action is?" He also made it clear that he would call me to witness, and that I would testify that "I had been beaten to the ground by officers." My

Catholic colleague, Father Peter Sammon of the Newman Center, would also be called to testify that he considered it in my proper line of duty as a Campus Pastor to be present on the campus with students and faculty to whom I was called to minister, just as it had been proper for the Catholic Chaplain for Police Officers to be present on the campus with the 600 police officers who were there that day to whom he was called to minister.

Too late I learned that trying to follow the challenge that my hero and model Martin Luther King had given to me four years earlier was not possible in this situation. I had hoped that what I had tried to do would be affirmed by this trial. Obviously it was a naive hope. Although I personally was committed to nonviolence, and had tried to counsel nonviolence to those who would listen to me, there had not been the training necessary for a committed group of students to lead a successful nonviolent action. Back in 1955 in Montgomery, Alabama, Rosa Parks had not suddenly decided to nonviolently refuse to go to the back of the bus, but had trained for nonviolent action for several years as part of a nonviolence program, and her action had led to the Montgomery Bus Boycott and the 1956 Supreme Court decision outlawing segregation on local bus lines. In 1960 young black college students didn't suddenly begin a nonviolent sit-in at a downtown lunch counter at Woolworth's in Greensboro, North Carolina, but had studied the philosophy and tactics of nonviolent protest carefully before their successful sit-in protest brought dramatic racial changes there and in many other southern cities. Nonviolent Direct Action leading to social change requires intense training before it can be effective. Therefore, my efforts, and the efforts of others in campus ministry, together with students and faculty who also shared a nonviolent commitment, were overwhelmed by forces ready to use tactics of a violent nature. On one side was the anger of students protesting unjust campus conditions and wanting to change them. On the other side was the entrenched forces of the establishment, political and administrative, resisting efforts to bring about constructive change. Standing between such forces, trying to nonviolently assist in mediating a constructive, positive, just, peaceful resolution, had proven to be impossible

That trial ended suddenly after three weeks of jury selection when the Judge declared a mistrial. The district attorney had used his peremptory challenges to dismiss all ten blacks that had been called up. After the 6th black had been dismissed, our attorneys objected that blacks were being systematically excluded from the jury, although to no avail. Finally, after the tenth exclusion, our attorneys again objected. I personally, being unable to remain quiet any longer at the shame and hypocrisy of such tactics, jumped up and protested to the judge that: "I've preached against racism for twenty years as a Christian pastor in the church and on university campuses and cannot sit idly by without objecting to such obvious racism displayed in a court of justice." I was warned that such an outburst could result in contempt of court, nevertheless this was not simply an impulsive action, as it gave expression to my growing conviction after observing other trials relating to SFSU and then seeing the same discriminatory practices evolve in this case. At that point the Judge demanded the District Attorney answer this charge of deliberate discrimination against blacks. When the District Attorney refused to answer the charges, it was our hope that he would be held in contempt of court, the charges against us dropped, and most important, precedent be set insuring blacks of fairness in the courts and their rights for participating on juries. Unfortunately, none of this happened, only that a mistrial having been called, a new trial date would be set in the future.

More than two years later, in November of 1972, nearly four years after the incident of the arrest, the case was again finally to come to trial. My attorney's efforts for dismissal of the case had been opposed by the District Attorney's insistence that the case should go to trial. Finally, the judge agreed to accept a plea of 'nolo contender' (I would not contest the court's decision) in return for the dismissal of three charges and acceptance of guilt for one charge, 'failure to disperse', and a small fine. I had previously rejected two such offers, insisting on my innocence and also on exposing the racist policies of the District Attorney's office. However, on the advice of my attorney I finally agreed to accept the offer.

For me personally, the storm that had been gathering for a long time had finally fully spent itself. Its force had blown me in many directions. Having as a young man gone to war to bring peace, I had learned that war is not the way to peace, peace is the way. Having become a minister, thinking my task was to be a pastor to people, I had learned that a valid ministry required me to be not only a pastor, but also a prophet, trying to discern God's will for the world and then proclaiming it and putting one's life on the line to bring it about, no matter the opposition, no matter how unpopular it might be. Having gone to Africa to teach and minister to others, I discovered my own American parochialism as they taught me 'ujamaa' and 'uhuru', true togetherness and community and true freedom. Having thought I had become an educated man by getting a bachelor degree, a masters degree, a doctors degree, and spending years as a student, a professor, a chaplain, a campus pastor and a congregational pastor, I finally realized that most of what I had most profitably learned came from experiences, experiences that I had often resisted. Having learned that if we want peace, we must work for justice. Having seen the worst of bureaucracy in some University Trustees and a university President, in a Governor, in some academicians and some ministers, and too many of the general population, I also had been inspired by Tanzanian President Nyerere, by my friend and pastor Hal, by my hero King, by the bravery of Bishop Segerhammer, by some black students who had the courage to stand tall for justice, by some white students who too were ready to work for a more just world, by many faculty risking tenure, by newsmen who insisted on reporting the unpopular truth, by the leaders of my own Lutheran Church and as well as many other denominations who gave me strong support in the face of much critical public opinion, and by dozens of lay people and fellow pastors who were on the same journey as I. The storm had truly been a blessing for me in my journey. Now the journey was to continue in new directions.

My arrest nearly four years earlier had left a lasting personal experience of the violent use of state socially approved power by the establishment to destroy legitimate and constructive educational, racial, and social change at that university.

My faith, the life perspective with which I as a Christian view the world, made much difference in all this. Personally, the wild, fiery,

Jerry Pedersen

tender, gentle, radical love of the Holy One, which vibrantly shines in the face of the Cosmic Christ, and passionately and humanly radiates from the man Jesus, has been the reason for me not turning either cynical or bitter, but remaining hopeful, expectant, committed to announcing Gospel, Good News, to the world and working towards its fulfillment and redemption.

"If you want peace, work for justice."

—*Pope Paul VI*

JERRY WITH
KIDS IN MEXICO
WORKSHOP
PROJECT
(RIGHT)

JERRY AND NICARAGUAN COUPLE AT
WITNESS FOR PEACE

JERRY AND
FATHER
AFTER
COMMUNION

WORSHIP SUNDAY AT MOUNT OF OLIVES LUTHERAN
CHURCH, MISSION VIEJO, CA

FARM WORKER
MINISTRY DIRECTOR
AND LEADERS WITH
JERRY AND
DIRECTOR OF LOPP
AT STATE CAPITOL
(LEFT)

JERRY ADMIRING
CHE MEMORIAL

DR. PEDERSEN IN HIS
STUDY AT MOUNT OF
OLIVES LUTHERAN
CHURCH

Chapter 7

<hr>

1970—2000: Dealing With the Storm's Aftermath

WHEN THE NEW UNIVERSITY year started at San Francisco State University following its longest student strike in the nation's history, the administration's Student Activity Office became concerned about the quality of student life. To my surprise, a few weeks into the first term, its Director phoned me at Ecumenical House asking me to come over to his office on the campus for a talk.

When we met, the Director told me he was concerned that students didn't seem to want to be involved in student government, the Gator campus newspaper, or other student activities. Hearing this from him, I could only laugh in disbelief and sick of heart. What had they expected? The Trustees had fired President Smith, who had the support of the faculty and was making progress in listening to the students and trying to find a constructive solution to the problems on campus. The Trustees had then imposed President Hayakawa on the university over faculty objections and student rejection, and Hayakawa had then taken militant actions that resulted in the loss of freedom for students and faculty, cutbacks and restricted funding for campus activities, and loss of student leadership. Under these circumstances, I told the Director, without change from the President and his policies on campus life, I knew of no way to help. I then suggested the Director arrange a meeting between the President and our Campus Ministry, since he held the power and we held ideas and desire to assist the University, and together we might begin the renewal needed. Unfortunately, the

President had earlier refused the offer of my Bishop to bring us together, and continued his opposition to our cooperation.

It wasn't only the University and its students and faculty that had been affected by the storm, it had touched me also. When President Hayakawa falsely accused me and Ecumenical House of being the fomenters of the troubles at SFSU and tried to pressure my Bishop to remove me from my ministry there, I found myself spending much of my time meeting and talking to community groups and congregations explaining the reality of the troubles at SFSU, contrary to public opinion formed by his manipulation of the media. Fortunately, my Bishop, my Campus Council, the area pastors, many congregations, the national church, and most faculty and students stood solidly supporting me. However, doing the ministry under the conditions of administration intimidation and the general publics distrust became increasingly discouraging.

Therefore, when the opportunity came for a year of post-doctoral study and research abroad, funded by grants from The Danforth Foundation and The Lutheran World Federation, I eagerly accepted it. I chose to pursue the year at the London School of Economics and Political Science, even though LSE and others suggested Kings College probably would be a better place for me, since it was where most theological students went. I insisted that I wanted this to be inter-disciplinary research, and feeling that I was well grounded in theological preparation, I wanted the emphasis to be on the social science dimension. In my proposal I stated that it was my growing conviction:

> "That society itself must assume greater responsibility for ordering its social and economic life, by determining goals of development and the means for reaching them, rather than leaving them almost blindly to private self-interest which excludes many from decision making, exercise of power or proportionate benefit. I have found myself asking whether European experiences with Democratic Socialism offer an alternative to either Democratic Capitalism of the USA (based on greed, exploitation, and personal freedom which is socially impotent) or Socialistic Communism (with its tendency

toward rigid dogmatic ideology, coercive elitism and bureaucracy)? How do we enable meaningful, radical, and constructive change to take place which increasingly means limiting the power of the defenders of the status quo, who manipulate the state and social instruments of control to maintain their advantage when possible, and launch out in violence to put down the aspirations of the majority when that becomes necessary? And what is the church's responsibility toward helping society formulate social policy in the interest of the many rather than in the self-interest of the few?"

My most specific investigation was into the National Health Service envisioned and developed in Britain. In the U.S. the American Medical Association (AMA) had successfully fought to keep public health in private hands, had attacked all opposition as 'bureaucratic interference with sacred rights of the American home' or 'tendency to promote communism' or 'socialized medicine' or 'the fight against government control of medicine'. In Britain, the fight was whether decent medical care is a basic right, like the right to food, shelter, clothing and education. The creation and revisions of the National Health Service (NHS) immediately following World War II and continuing over the following twenty years provided an illuminating example of how pressure groups influence social policy. In Britain, as elsewhere, social policies do not come down inscribed on sacred tablets from some political party, government, the medical profession, or idealistic reformer. I learned they come about through complicated discussion and negotiation facing political reality.

Criticism of the NHS certainly existed, though contrary to much popular American opinion (manipulated by American propagandists, primarily the AMA) I came to the conclusion that the NHS must be considered a success, and that the vast majority of British doctors and laity approve it. Originally fought by the British Medical Association, the BMA finally came to accepting the NHS, although its attitude was one of insuring doctors against the patient's inability to pay rather than insuring patients against the high cost of medical care. I came to the conclusion that my chief criticism of the NHS was its inability to get a higher percentage of the gross national product of the country allotted to health care. In 1961 Britain had been spending only 3.6% of its GNP on health care, compared to 6.6% in the USA. Since then it had gradually increased so that by 1970 the GNP there had risen to 4.7%. (Over the next thirty years the percentage spending in each country had nearly doubled, but the U.S. still was spending nearly twice as much of its GNP on health care compared with Britain.) The problem of allocation of precious, scarce resources (money, whether in taxes or in private spending, is always "scarce") is one of the chief problems confronting a nation which tries to deliberately and rationally decide on its social policy, rather than be subject to individual whim or to the market. The latter decision, taken by the U.S., is our response to the pressure of special interests, and offers no solution to the inequalities inherent in our national health care. The British made a deliberate decision to reject the 'Poor Law' rational that had existed for over a century, that applicants for relief give up all claims to equality with their fellows in society, that they should carry the stigma of the semi-criminal, and that in no case should their living conditions be on an equal standard with the lowest paid laborer. The Poor Laws had maintained that recipients of relief should suffer severe civil penalties, and had as its ethical rational that poverty itself demonstrated a personal failing, and that relief simply compounded the moral failing of the recipient and contributed to the breakdown of society and the economic system. Although the British rejected the assumptions of the 'poor law", in the U.S. those assumptions too often are still held, if unconsciously, by many who reject adequate health care for all citizens as a right, and not for only those who have the wealth to pay for it.

At the end of the year as I headed back home, I tried to rethink and evaluate my own journey through life, especially the quest for peace, my ministry, my personal faith and my commitments. The importance of community became a dominant concern. How do we move toward that 'Beloved Community' that King talked about? Is the reality of 'Ujamaa' that I had observed in East Africa a possibility in America? Is the Catholic and Anglican emphasis on the 'Common

*Good' that I heard so much about in Britain the key to peace to which
I was committed? Is genuine 'community' even possible in the highly
individualistic culture of American Capitalism, or under increasing
American Corporate dominance? Specifically, how do we move
the churches to a more responsible social theology, moving beyond
traditional private moral issues, to a communitarian social theology
concerned with building community, reforming worldly institutions,
seeking economic, racial, gender, and international justice, and
especially ending militancy and violence so as to approach a more
peaceful world?*

Returning to the States, I soon felt that SFSU was not the place
for me to continue my journey, and decided to move on. After
seriously considered an inner city, multi-racial and multi-cultural,
university related situation that seemed a challenging opportunity
for what I wished to pursue, upon closer examination it became
apparent that local resistance and restrictions in that particular
place were so dominant that all my efforts would be like knocking
my head against a wall. I kept hearing in my heart and mind the
words that an angry black student had said to me when he heard I
was considering leaving SFSU: "If you want to do something about
the problems of race and poverty, go out to the suburbs and attack
the problem, that's where all the power is!" When the opportunity
came to lead a congregation in a largely white, middle class, semi-
affluent new community in the middle of Orange County, perhaps
the most conservative county in California, a county that was
the center for the radical right John Birch Society, I accepted the
challenge. In an initial meeting with a dozen, mostly younger,
leaders of the congregation, I was surprised when they seemed
open to my description of what I wanted to do if called there, and
asked that I speak to the entire congregation.

However, fully expecting that when the entire membership of
this 5-year old congregation heard of my intentions, they would say
"no way". Not wanting to get caught in a situation where resistance
to my intentions would be so great that failure would be guaranteed,
I decided to strongly state those intentions in the so called "trial
sermon" a few weeks later before the entire congregation. Sharing
my faith, centered in the unconditional love and costly grace of

God, I said that such a faith enables us to freely follow the way Jesus lived and taught, seeking peace and justice for all and respecting one another in our diversity. Knowing at the center of your being that nothing can separate you from the love of God, it just doesn't matter what people say or do to you, you are free to give and love without fear.

To illustrate what I believed this meant for our lives, I suggested a number of things. Perhaps the women should change the nature of a week-end retreat that they would attend in a couple weeks, and instead go up to Delano and support the grape strike that Cesar Chavez and the farm workers were conducting, being willing to face the violence the workers were facing, and perhaps being arrested and put in jail even as the farm workers were. They should expect that I would oppose the violence of war, even as I opposed the war in Vietnam, and that I would advocate the right of Conscientious Objection to war, and urge youth to consider being COs. I mentioned the issues in education, reminding them of my involvement at SFSU. Although many people had condemned me for having been arrested there for disobeying a law, I believed it right to disobey man's law if it contradicted God's law, and that perhaps one shouldn't apologize for having been arrested or in jail, just as Peter, or Paul, or Martin Luther King, were—or for that matter, Jesus. Perhaps more Christians who had never been arrested should apologize, since society fell so far short of Christian or humanitarian standards. Needless to say, I really didn't expect them to vote to call me as their pastor, and told my wife she didn't need to worry about packing for a move.

While I was in Chicago a week later exploring other options, my wife received a phone call, and to her surprise they said they wanted me there in Orange County. Later, after several phone calls, I asked if there was opposition to my coming, and they truthfully told me, yes there was opposition, however it was a very small minority, and the large majority of people were excited about the possibility for an engaged and vigorous ministry. Only later was I told that several of the 'biggest givers' voiced serious objections and soon left the congregation, while several others had "deep reservations" but were willing to give me a chance. In later years, two of the 'deep reservation' people had become among my best friends and supporters, although still disagreeing about many things—an attitude I deeply respected and consider an essential aspect of the kind of community I so deeply wanted—the beginnings of '*Ujamaa*', of '*The Beloved Community*', even of a '*Communitarian Social Theology*'. Ever since reading in college Arnold Toynbee's '*A Study of History*' I had been intrigued by his idea of the "Creative minority", and I was hopeful that our spiritual community might be of that quality.

I was often thankful of having laid out my priorities with no punches pulled in the very beginning. Continuing there nearly twenty years before retiring, many times people had complained of what they considered my radical ways, though I was careful to explain that from the beginning it had been very clear what I would do and say. Often I had suggested to such people that perhaps they would be happier in a different religious community, since such congregations surrounded us. Typically they would answer, "No, we like this congregation, it's so vibrant and joyful and alive". It would then be suggested that it might be that way because people agreed to disagree while respecting differences, or because our spirituality was deeply immersed in confronting moral social issues contrary to the prevailing culture and fundamentalists preoccupation with private individualistic morality, or that we considered following the way of Jesus as more important than strictly adhering to doctrinal beliefs.

Two months after beginning there, we had the National Farm Worker Ministry chaplain speak to the congregation, explaining why Christians felt compelled to advocate for improvement of working conditions for field hands. This was followed by a delegation spending three days at Keene Ranch, headquarters for UFW. Meeting Cesar Chavez and experiencing the spiritual basis for his efforts on behalf of field workers led the delegation to committing full support for '*La Huelga*' (the strike) and '*La Causa*' (the cause or struggle). Personally, I shall never forget his saying to us: "We are only just beginning to understand the power of love because we are just beginning to understand the weakness of force and oppression." I recognized that I indeed had much to learn about the power of love, and that I still had much to learn about the weakness of force. I resolved right then to make this a priority in my 'quest for peace'.

Upon our return, we had people walking the picket lines in front of local grocery stores, with signs supporting the 'grape strike'. One women picketing was spit upon, and my wife experienced being called 'a dirty communist'. A phone caller to our church office complained about its pastor being on a picket line. One of our members moved to the strike area for several years to be an educator and do public relations for the strike. It was many years later before we threw a party celebrating the acceptability of drinking 'Gallo wine' again, although there had always been those who had objected to our support of the strike, and had continually delighted in making the point by serving the 'forbidden fruit'.

As the Vietnam War was finally winding down, those of us in the Lutheran Peace Fellowship in California, having opposed that war because it failed to meet any criteria of a 'Justifiable War', organized a Lutheran Peace Symposium seeking to prevent such a war from happening in the future. Peace Fellowships from many other Christian and other Religious Fellowships were encouraged to conduct such efforts at this time. We scheduled ours to take place twice, each at different campuses, a week apart, in Berkeley at Pacific Lutheran Theological Seminary, and in the south at California Lutheran College. Serving as organizer for both symposiums, I was able to have a large delegation from my congregation participate in the second one, with the result that we had a core group of peace activists to energize our future peace efforts. We had sections on the Psychological, Economic, and Political Causes and Resources for Peace, and A Christian Theology For Our Day. In the aftermath of the Vietnam War our efforts were to recognize that the ethical position called 'Justifiable War' of the Lutheran Church and most other Christian Churches was untenable in our current modern world.

Following the Symposium, I edited the tapes and papers from the presentations and had them published in book form titled "*Peace—On Not Leaving It to the Pacifists*". In it I called for our reconsideration of the pacifist position, which had too often been understood only from a negative standpoint—a rejection of killing and war. It is that. But it is primarily a aggressively pursued positive commitment to peace-building, toward building positive solutions in situations of conflict and toward developing positive relationships between individuals, groups and nations. It is less about what happens after war breaks out, than it is about what should happen long before war breaks out, hopefully so that war is avoided. As A.J. Muste had said, "there is no way to peace, peace is the way". Only then is peace possible, as a continuing process. I preferred not to use the pacifist label that is too easily misunderstood as simply a passive attitude toward violence. That was my original impression of pacifism that I had first encountered while in the Marine Corps—a passive, extremely idealistic and ineffectual idea. However, that was certainly not true for the pacifists I had come to know, who were exceedingly active in promoting nonviolent solutions to many social issues. It was at this point that I began a serious study of what I would eventually prefer to call "Active Nonviolence."

Increasingly I was discovering the wisdom of the current slogan "Think Globally, Act Locally". Based on my experiences and my studies, I became aware that my outlook on life was increasingly taking a 'global dimensions'. I could no longer consider the 'problems of the moment' without considering their 'long-term implications'. I was becoming increasingly aware that individuals and groups often thought and acted only out of 'self-interest' with little consideration for the 'common good'. Increasingly I no longer thought primarily as an 'American', but as a 'world citizen', no longer as a 'man' but as a 'human being', no longer primarily as a 'Lutheran', but as a 'Christian' or as a 'Spiritual' person. And, although I was confident that thinking and acting from this perspective was responsible and wise, I also was becoming aware that this was often causing problems and criticisms from many people who thought and acted out of a more restricted perspective. It was difficult to resist the temptation to quickly judge such people as wrong or mean-spirited or just plain ignorant—although it is possible that for some of them it might be true. I had to keep reminding myself that I had been on this journey toward thinking globally for a long time, and in fact was still on it. Without the privileges I had been fortunate to enjoy for academic study and for worldly and spiritual experiences, I might have been the same as these people who did not have the advantages I had. This non-judgmental attitude was part of the nonviolent attitude I needed to develop further. I also needed to find ways to help others think and act globally.

As long as I could remember, I had been practicing a degree of altruism. It may have begun when I was a Boy Scout and took seriously the motto 'Be Prepared' and 'Do a Good Turn Daily'. My journey through life had taken me from trying to live responsibly in my immediate surroundings toward growing responsible also in larger settings, or globally, and helping others to do the same. Now I found myself needing to also emphasize the other half of the truth "Think Globally, Act Locally". This led me to the Interfaith Peace Ministry (IPM) of Orange County. Here I found a way to seek peace not only globally, but also specifically where I was living, in Orange County. Likewise, I found a way to participate not only as part of my Christian community, but also as part of the broader interfaith community.

As part of IPM we did everything from locally planting a 'Peace Pole' in parks and civic centers and churches throughout our county, to globally opposing militarism, military spending, the arms race, intervention in Central America and nuclear armaments. We discovered peace among ourselves in this inclusive community even as in working for peace we discovered fresh dimensions to peace. We knew that peace was not just the 'absence of war', or 'deterrent strength', and always had to remind ourselves that "if we want peace, we must work for justice", for there is no peace where poverty prevailed or injustice reigned. Our Vision of Peace required us to work to change the status quo as controlled by wealth and power, and work to stop environmental deterioration. And we discovered that each of the major faiths had at it deepest heart a dream and vision of peace which was a dynamic, harmonious, life-affirming humanity and created order. And although we knew that religions all too often failed to live out their dream of peace, we also knew that the power and inspiration of spiritual faith was essential for achieving justice and peacemaking. Therefore, we persevered in our peace actions together, experiencing joy and peace among ourselves in our very inclusive community. We took seriously Hans Kung's saying: "There will be no peace among the nations without peace among the religions."

This "Thinking Globally, Acting Locally" needed to be taken seriously in our congregation. Before my coming to the congregation, they had begun sponsorship of an orphanage in Baja, Mexico. Each year the associate pastor took High School youth, together with a massive amount of building supplies and equipment, and spent a week or two 90 miles south of the border assisting with care, teaching, and playing with the orphans. It was a great program for the benefit of the orphanage children, and also for our youth, who came home appreciating how fortunate they were here in the states. My concern was that it too easily contributed to a paternalistic feeling on our part: 'Just look at what wonderful things we are doing for those unfortunate people'. This had been a too common experience that I had witnessed in my time in Africa blinding us to the detrimental effect of colonialism on its people, and especially on trade relationships that colonialists controlled that worked to the advantage of the colonialists and to the disadvantage of the Africans. I was determined to use and keep the previous program going, but while beginning efforts to educate people to a better understanding of the neo-colonialism developing on the part of first world countries in relationship to the third world.

To prepare myself for this task, I was able to take three months of vacation and sabbatical time for study and travel. I decided first to visit 'The Cuernavaca Center for Intercultural Dialogue on Development' (CCIDD) in Mexico. CCIDD advocated that American Christians needed to:

> "Conscienticize themselves to the reality that many unjust structures which emanate from their own country are key causes of the poverty and underdevelopment of Latin America, and to act to influence their own nation which is in a central position to bring about structural change for global justice rather than continuing the unjust status quo of which it is very much a part."

Spending two weeks at CCIDD visiting squatters settlements, rural Indian villages, talking to poor people and visiting their homes, dialoging with factory workers, Mexican women and many others helped me to see reality through their eyes. Talking to university professors, union leaders, government officials and exiled priests interpreting United States involvement with their problems helped me to understand the theology of liberation and interdependence and solidarity in the struggle for human liberation.

This experience convinced me that upon returning I needed to get a core of our congregation to take part in the CCIDD program. Hopefully, that would help create the creative minority in our congregations needed for us to most effectively work for reducing poverty in other countries, and in America. Therefore we had the director of CCIDD come and speak to our congregation, and for several years we took ten to fifteen people each year to the CCIDD program. Upon returning, they helped educate others by presenting slides and discussions to small group gatherings in homes. Without the support of this creative minority, it would have been difficult to continue my efforts toward conscienticization.

Following my experience at CCIDD I was able to spend a month in Central American countries and Columbia and Ecuador. I spent two weeks visiting the school, vocational training center and community garden experiment in Ecuador that a friend, Jan, had established. Following several years in the Peace Corps, she had continued working with the same people in one of the poorest rural areas in the country. Jan would come back to California, travel for two months on her motorcycle loaded down with all her provisions and sleeping bag, visiting congregations who supported her work there, twice speaking to our congregation and inspiring us with her efforts. She had often requested for someone from the States to come visit the project, not only to validate to others her work there, but even more importantly for the people there to be encouraged by actually seeing an American Christian who supported and was interested in them. I was embarrassed by their awe and attention to me, and I doubt that the President or the Pope or our Bishop could have impressed them more. The sewing class made a shirt for me, the welding students demonstrated their welding skills, and the women of the community garden described how learning better scientific and agricultural practices had enriched their family diets. I'm sure my time with them, living in the same housing conditions they lived in, eating their food, and learning of their lives did more to enhance American relationships than all our government's efforts, at least for these several hundred Ecuador rural poor people.

Traveling in Nicaragua and Guatemala, I met a friend in Guatemala City that I had known in California that was now working there. He invited me to attend a dinner invitation with him the next evening at a private home with people from the large Protestant American Church. I eagerly accepted the invitation. Picking me up in his car, we drove out to a very exclusive area of homes. Pulling up to the driveway, I noted the high concrete wall with broken pieces of glass embedded at the top. A guard opened the locked gate and we parked amid four luxury cars, and entered a most luxurious home. Five gentlemen greeted us. In conversation during the fabulous dinner I learned that one was a high level person in the U.S. Embassy, two were CEOs of large pharmaceutical companies, and the other two were businessmen, and all were Americans. My friend made a decided point of informing them of my Marine Corps background, my doctorate and university experiences, and foreign overseas service. They in turn told me of the hardships of living in a Latin American country, the difficulty of doing business there but also the high profits and advantageous tax and trade advantages for Americans. After dinner my friend quietly informed me that this informal evening was, in fact, arranged by them to conduct an informal 'pastoral call' committee interview for the vacant position of Senior Pastor for the American Protestant Church there. He was sure they were considering me a prime candidate and were seriously considering me for the position. Although I had at one time considered serving again overseas, I realized that this situation would be totally unacceptable to me. When we reassembled, I began sharing my experiences at CCIDD, in Ecuador and Nicaragua, and my experiences in East Africa and in the student strike at SFSU, my rejection of the Vietnam War and especially my criticism of our U. S. foreign policy in Latin America. I was amused to see their enthusiasm for the possibility of extending a call to me sink lower and lower and then totally vanish. When I suggested they should spend a week or two at CCIDD in order to better serve the Guatemalan people and help change American foreign policy and trade relationships, it became apparent that our evening was finished. I still cannot help having a hearty laugh every time I recall that evening.

The final two weeks ending my 3-month travel-study sabbatical was spent in Cuba traveling with a group of American university professors and campus pastors. We had arranged to leave from Mexico City, since it was illegal to go there from the states. Although we used the Cuban travel bureau to help arrange our itinerary, contrary to public opinion in the states, we were able to make our own arrangements for where we went and whom we spoke to. For example, I and another fellow spent one entire day in Havana, talking to people at the University, in small stores and on the streets, walking along the El Malecon Habanero, and going to Ernest Hemingway's favorite La Bodeguita del Medio Bar, and in the evening attending a downtown nightclub, without any interference or unpleasant incidents. Another day we spent at the 'United Protestant Seminary' talking to students and faculty, hearing their opinions and criticisms and praises of Cuban life and church issues and theological thought. Other times the group interviewed people in labor unions, government offices, large and small businesses, farmers, housing cooperatives and other situations, and experienced no government interference.

We spent an entire afternoon with a member of the Communist Party Central Committee, the Minister for Education, Culture and Religion. He told us of his heritage. He was born into a wealthy family that had often vacationed abroad, owned several homes in Havana and at the beach, and he like his sisters and brother had been educated in France and the U.S., and he had become a successful lawyer. Later he joined the Communist Party and supported the Revolution because he believed corruption by the ruling class kept the masses powerless and in poverty without any chance of improving their condition. Now, he said, that although most Cubans still lived very poor lives, at least they had food to eat, a guaranteed job, representation in the government, and most importantly, hope for the future. That he no longer had access to several houses and vacations abroad and the other privileges he formerly enjoyed he willingly accepted, he said, for the sake of all the Cuban people. He agreed that the present situation of the country under communism was far from ideal, although much better than the pre-revolutionary capitalistic days under the U.S. supported Bautista government, even though the country was still in the preliminary stage of the process toward true socialism. I was very impressed by him, and was able to test the validity of some of what he told us as we later visited and interviewed other Cubans.

He apologized for the fact that wage differentials between the richer and poorer were still in the neighborhood of four or five to one, whereas the goal was to achieve a more justifiable differential of two or three to one, but that this kind of change had such economic and political implications that it would take time to achieve. He suggested that what was happening in Cuba offered a much more hopeful model of development and democracy than the model America supported in the rest of Latin America. I remember feeling embarrassed as I realized how few of our people apologize for the far wider wage and income differentials between rich and poor in our own country. In later years, as these differentials in America grew increasingly larger and larger, I not only felt embarrassment but also anger.

The medical clinics we visited were very simple compared to ours, yet when we talked to people using them we heard stories of how thrilled they were to have such facilities for the first time in their lives. Likewise, not all doctors had the degree of training that we require in the states. However, it was true that people in all walks in life, many of them for the first time in their lives, even the poorest and those in rural areas, had access to basic medical care and cost was not a factor.

The Bureaucracy of social organization was especially evident. For example, in the cities the neighborhoods were organized to see that the elderly had care, children were in school, the sick could get to the clinic, and even that each family had some kind of vacation each year. Each neighborhood, as small as a block or more, elected their own leaders and representatives, who might deal with matters as local as disputes between two residents or as citywide as police matters. Rural areas and vocational groupings were also similarly organized. However, whereas I had the feeling that in the USA most instances of bureaucracy, whether in our institutions, or businesses, or in government, power came from the top down, whereas in Cuba I had the feeling that bureaucracy had more the character of power coming from the bottom up.

Upon returning home after three months, I continually heard conditions in Cuba being compared to conditions in the USA. Whether the comparison was their standard-of-living, the luxury of hospitalization, the amount of Freedom or whatever, Cuba usually rated poorly, or in the minds of most people, disastrously. However, that comparison is unrealistic and unfair. Every country south of us in the Americas would rate poorly in most categories compared to us. However, when compared to other countries in Latin America, Cuba would rate very favorably with any of them, and superior to most of them. Compared to their nearest neighbors, Haiti and Santo Domingo, they rate vastly superior.

When taking into account that much of Cuba's wealth, educated leaders, doctors, and yes even their priests and pastors, had left the country following the Revolution, not because they were forced to leave, but because they refused to give up control of the advantages they reveled in by suppressing the majority of the population, it was amazing that Cuba had been able to make the progress it had made. Likewise, when I remember that the USA, which had historically been Cuba's chief trading partner and our tourists a primary source of revenue for their economy, had cut them off from our trade, refused to allow our citizens to travel there, and had even assisted those who sought to overthrow their government, I was amazed that they had survived at all, let alone that they had made progress. I came away ashamed for our country's treatment of them.

I was surprised shortly after returning from Cuba to be challenged to be the bible study leader for several hundred women at a Lutheran Woman's Convention. They asked me to use the theme based on Romans 1:12 "that we may be mutually encouraged by each other's faith, both yours and mine". After first reminding them of my reputation, I accepted. These were to be three hour long presentations over three days, and I decided to base my presentation on my three experiences of "mutual encouragement" in the African country of Tanzania, in Central and South America, and in Cuba. Although I was happy about the "encouragement" I had given to the people in those countries, I realized they also had given me as much "encouragement" or more.

The first day I spoke of Tanzania where the people taught me 'ujamaa'—true community, togetherness and family. I compared this to our Western individualism taking precedence over our commitment to community. Even our congregations tend to be mere collections of individuals with little understanding of being communities, 'one body'. The second day I spoke of meeting with people of Ecuador, Columbia and Guatemala in '*communidades de base*' (Small Base Communities), as they studied the scriptures and discovered the distinction between 'charity' and 'justice'. They learned that in Exodus Moses did not ask Pharaoh for 'charity', such as a little more food. Rather, Moses challenged the institutional injustice of the system, that the Jewish forced-labor camps be ended, that unjust Egyptian laws be disobeyed, and ultimately led his people to freedom. They read in Jeremiah that to "know God is to do justice". I suggested that perhaps Jesus said "blessed are the poor" because reading scripture through the eyes of the poor enables them to see truth, whereas reading scripture through the eyes of the rich blinds them to the truth. I then asked whether this might also be true for us affluent Americans. Whereas the first day I sensed unanimous appreciation of what I had said, I sensed that on this second day I began encountering resistance from a few.

Finally, the third day I spoke of experiences in Communist Cuba. I told them that had I come directly from the USA I might not have been quite so impressed, since they were so much less developed than our country. However having come directly from Guatemala, the contrast was decidedly in Cuba's favor. Employment—all were guaranteed jobs, although not up to our standards, whereas a third of Guatemalans were unemployed. Food to eat—although people lacked much of what we enjoyed, all had basics, compared to Guatemalans 50% below nutritional standards. Education—all children went at least to the 8th grade, with the goal of high school to be achieved soon, compared to 30% of Guatemalans never entering school at all. Medical—all had access to medical care, with an oversupply of doctors, to the extent many were serving in other undeveloped countries. Even more importantly, I said, I had witnessed the pride in the progress they were making toward an egalitarian society, and dignity that comes from hope in a better future. And among Christians, they spoke in biblical terms about the 'new age', the 'new man', the 'new society', not motivated by greed and acquisition as in capitalist countries, but as part of the 'new community', the 'Kingdom of God', and their concern for the 'least among them'.

When I finished, a small number of women were angered by this study, questioning my patriotism and my faith, though I was surprised and pleased that overwhelmingly the others indicated approval and appreciation. I received invitations to come to a number of congregations. Later, I was asked to lead the leadership of this group in an exploration in Mexico toward better understanding of poverty, third world problems and their relationship to our United States trade and investment policies. I considered my time well spent.

In leading my congregation I always felt some pressure and the temptation to compromise my convictions regarding my faith, and to compromise my peace and justice efforts in order to accommodate living in our American culture of affluence. I discovered that I would have been highly rewarded if I simply followed 'going along' doing what many people in our culture expected. I determined to resist doing this, and fortunately our congregation kept growing, building larger facilities and increasing our staff even though I continually pushed a very liberal agenda. However, when I pushed too hard 'comforting the afflicted, while afflicting the comfortable' there was always some resistance. A local newspaper ran an article with a headline:

> "Pastor Makes Congregation Squirm—
> He preaches radical, serious sermons...has been called
> unpatriotic and un-American... He came to Orange
> County fifteen years ago to prick the consciences of

the area's affluent residents—the types of people who determine the policies and values of our nation...he weaves themes of social responsibly into sermons... true spirituality must be applied to social as well as personal issues...social change is threatening to people who have found a comfortable niche in the status quo... he gets many complaints, many leave... why does his congregation grow? He says because people want to know the truth, even when it hurts... but his serious message has joy at its center—he says 'dare to dance in the midst of life' and that if you want to take a prophetic stance in life, you better express a joyful outlook."

During the '80s I tried to put together a coherent plan to integrate my resistance to our prevailing culture and for taking global responsibility for poverty here and in the third world, as an expression of my Christian faith and its ethical demands. At one level, in attempting to help people gain a world perspective, I led groups of people on explorations of Israel, Palestine, and Egypt, and another to China. However, my experience in these was disappointing. Unlike my use of social justice immersion workshops that we would later conduct in poor urban, rural, and inner-city areas in California and Mexico, these experiences seldom got much beyond the 'ugly American tourist' awareness of poverty and injustice. These experiences, together with Martin Luther King's 'Nonviolent Direct Action' and Gustavo Gutierrez's 'Liberation Theology', helped me toward a better understanding of our situation as similar to the Biblical story of the Exodus.

We also were living in our Egypt, our affluent society, and those of us in the middle class were neither poor nor did we belong to the power elite, but too often had adapted ourselves to living an Egyptian lifestyle, living in Pharaoh's court. And the poor of the Third World were like the slaves in Egypt. I could no longer reconcile the injustice of the present reality here and abroad with my faith, and was determined to encourage a creative minority within the congregation to also be unwilling to reconcile the present system of injustice with their faith and their theology. I encouraged people to think of my task, not as 'pastoral', adjusting to the present situation, but as 'prophetic', resisting the present situation and seeking to change it. And changing the concept of 'salvation' from being oriented to future-world fulfillment, to its original and more Biblical meaning 'liberation', deliverance to a present world reality where peace and justice would actually be possible. This meant seeing Christ not so much as 'Savior' who comes down from above to salvage us and remove us from our situation in which we are victims and can do nothing, and instead seeing Christ as 'Liberator' who is part of a movement of liberation in which Christ and people cooperate together in the 'struggle' for a more just world. And participation in this 'struggle' for a more just and therefore more peaceful world is essential for Christians. Not to participate in the 'struggle' is to consent to the status quo, the situation of our Egypt – Pharaoh, the slaves, and those in Pharaoh's Court, us! Not to participate in the 'struggle' of liberation is to oppose the Exodus. This was the rational for what I was trying to do in this congregation, and in all my interactions with society.

Therefore, I was determined to begin an experiment to help individuals become a community to achieve these goals. We called this an experiment in 'Radical Christianity', or 'Radical Discipleship' or 'Small Base Community in Our Affluent Society'. Together with several others, we invited members and friends to join this experiment. I wrote: "For some time I've been pondering two questions—How do we help persons grow toward spiritual maturity? And how does a congregation really become a true community of disciples following Jesus? I invite you to share in an experiment trying to answer these questions, and to what could be a life changing sharing-in-community experience as a disciple of Jesus that eventuates in a fresh understanding of Christ's church."

We had hoped for a larger number of people taking advantage of this experimental attempt to form in our affluent American society a parallel to the *'communidades de base'*, the base or grassroots communities of Latin America. However, it was a beginning and a serious step toward individual growth leading to a small-group community, and as precursor of a creative minority and global community. M. Scott Peck, M.D., author of *'The Road Less Traveled'*, said that only one in five Christians ever get beyond the lowest level of faith, and fewer yet ever reach a truly mature faith in following the way of Jesus. We were hopeful of raising that percentage.

We discovered that many of us in our affluent society were so absorbed in our culture that we were blind to the reality of our situation. Whereas most people in our area thought only the few at the top of our financial world were 'rich', or that America was the 'most generous nation' on earth, the reality was that most of us are 'rich' if measured against the majority of people in the world, and our nation ranked far down the list in generosity if measured by the percentage of our giving to poorer countries. I often asked adults in Bible Studies whether the actual words of Jesus used in the Beatitudes were Matthew's "Blessed are the *poor in spirit*'" or Luke's "Blessed are the *poor*'". Most thought the words of Matthew were the actual words of Jesus because they thought Jesus was speaking of 'spiritual reality', not 'material reality'. Then I would tell them most biblical scholars insisted Luke's "Blessed are the *poor*'" were the actual words, based on the fact that most of the people Jesus normally talked to were materially 'poor' and that his words "good news to the 'poor'" elsewhere consistently referred to material poverty. Even then many in the class would continue arguing that Jesus must have really been talking about 'spiritual poverty', otherwise his message would not be "good news" for us in our affluence. "Ah-ha" I would say, "That realization is exactly the point!" the starting point of taking the bible seriously, of taking Jesus seriously, and the starting point on the road to a mature faith.

Many people, including the people in this congregation, are good, well-intentioned folks, serious about their faith, while practicing a privatized religion—unrelated to the world. They relegate Jesus to the domain of inner consciousness, losing the compelling qualities inherent in the life of Jesus. Their religion is personal, but also private. Our intention was to help 'radicalize' their faith, that is, to go to the roots of what Jesus taught and lived—a faith that has both inner and outer expressions, both personal and societal, both individual and communal. Our intention was to develop a community of radicalized discipleship. It had three parts, all closely related to each other. First, developing radicalized attitudes toward and commitments to the real world in which we live. Second, sharing in a small community exploring these attitudes and commitments. Third, adopting new lifestyles, sharing in community relationships and involvement in concrete social actions. These three parts needed to happen simultaneously.

We approached our task of 'radicalizing discipleship' or 'radicalizing Christianity' as being neither doctrinal, the virtues commonly associated with discipleship, nor the qualities normally considered spiritual. Rather, our task was to develop new attitudes toward and commitment to the real world in which we live. People too often considered social, political and economic goals as not being relevant to religious goals, especially by people who had privatized or spiritualized following Jesus. Our approach started with the idea that loving God only becomes meaningful in actual situations, the way we love our neighbor, our enemy, and our world. Our discussions therefore led to considering six areas: What it meant— 1) Living in Solidarity with the Poor; 2) Living as Peacemakers; 3) Living Non-violently; 4) Living seeking Justice for All; 5) Living Ecologically Responsible Lives; and finally, 6) Living Gracefully in the Way of Community.

Using the insights of Liberation Theology as we sought to develop Small Base Communities Within an Affluent Society, we tried to resist the possibility that this would simply become another 'head trip' exercise. In addition to input of new ideas and factual information, each participant in the small base community was given some carefully selected outside reading to share, and were encouraged to discuss with each other critically the topics from not only their own experiences of powerlessness, frustrations, failures and successes, but also from the perspective of the oppressed and marginalized people of the Third World and from those in our own back yards. Developing a community where people truly respected one another, were non-judgmental in their attitudes, accepted responsibility for the goals of the community and were open minded toward new ideas and new relationships was an essential aspect of the process of community building.

The third part of our community process was putting our new insights and commitments into practice. This was to be both personal and social. We looked at how we prioritized our time, our budget, our meditation and study, and how our lifestyle influenced our commitments. Each participant also made a commitment to engage in some kind of specific social action—peacemaking, reducing poverty, working for economic equality, reducing environmental destruction, or whatever area they chose. However, we tried to benefit from the experiences of the Latin American 'communidades de base' that had exposed the fallacy in many good intended social actions, actions that simply condoned the present unjust order in society, and did not change anything. Such actions were simply tokenism, exploitative or paternalistic. Our actions needed to stand the test of overcoming injustice rather than perpetuating it. Liberation theology used the term 'praxis' to describe the ongoing interplay of reflection and action. Our actions were not to be done to serve our own ego needs or to be done unthinkingly lest they serve to perpetuate something unjust or downright evil. This reflective process evaluating our actions was an important aspect of our small base communities, perhaps even more essential in our affluent communities than in the 'communidades de base'.

Although we were never able to enlist a large number of people in this experimental 'Small Base Community in an Affluent Society', I considered the experiment a success! A significant number of individuals, sharing in a variety of small group arrangements, became a dynamic minority creative community working and bringing changes promoting peace and justice, and influencing the larger congregation of which it was a part and society in general. During the decade of the 80s and early 90s, those sharing in the community were involved in a wide variety of peace and justice efforts, always in their participation trying to reflect the community's view that oppression of the poor is intolerable, that discrimination toward others is scandalous, that violence can never be redemptive, and that there is no way to peace – for peace is the way.

For people not living in our immediate area I wanted to offer an experience here in the States similar to that which we had benefited from with CCIDD in Cuernavaca. Together with Joan, a dedicated colleague, we organized the California Center for Intercultural Justice and Creative Awareness, CCIJCA (pronounced SEEK-A) established for Christians and others who wanted to work for peace and help overcome poverty and hunger by correcting its root causes. We took as our theme, "If you want Peace, work for justice." Through experimental and intellectual involvement, we provided a consciousness-raising experience to create an awareness of the interdependence that exists in the quest for human liberation, whether people are poor or rich, a struggle that crosses all cultural and national borders. The program included exposure to poverty, affluence, oppression, consumerism and corporate life. The full program was for seven days, although alternatives were offered to meet particular needs, so that the majority were for either five days or two or three weekends.

The aim of the experience was to be exposed, firsthand, to the reality of poverty, its relationship to affluence, to hear expert interpretations of the experience, and to reflect with the group about each day's experience. We went to Los Angeles to visit Skid Row, soup kitchens, and welfare housing. In El Centro we witnessed farm worker ministry, the fields where they worked and the canyons where they slept outdoors. In San Diego we met the undocumented and saw the immigration process through their eyes. In Tijuana we visited squatter's settlements and the American plants exported there to the cheaper labor sources. Locally we visited large corporations and tried to analyze and evaluate the role of business in progress and oppression. We spent time discussing Latin America and American Policy, liberation theology, small base communities and global responsibilities. The experience we tried to offer was illustrated by the symbol on our brochure—a distorted globe, representing one world and all humanity, though distorted and elongated because of a lack of justice, and a white dove representing peace hovering over the darkened world—suggesting peace is possible where there is justice.

We limited the size of CCIJCA groups to ten or less, while some of the most effective had as few as four. Although we did accept some participation by lone individuals, we encouraged participation by groups of four or more from a congregation or a community to better enable their efforts to act on their experiences once they returned home. We tried to keep in touch with those who had participated, offering encouragement, knowing how easy it is to get discouraged in an affluent society with misplaced priorities, where personal charity for the well-being of a few is grossly ineffective without recognizing the systems of destruction and oppression that enslave so many and in the midst of our idolatry of national sovereignty. We wanted them to know that we at CCIJCA were committed, and counted on them as Christian and Humanitarian activists, to speak and act and intelligently organize for Shalom. Fortunately, we received reports of groups that went home and organized adult and youth classes, got involved in justice projects in their communities, and cooperated with local interfaith efforts toward poverty reduction in their communities. Individuals who had taken part reported making career justice vocational choices, and others reported developing life style changes as a result of participating in our CCIJCA program. Although we were encouraged by the successes of our CCIJCA program, we had to acknowledge that it was very difficult to get people in an affluent society to covenant together to simplify their lifestyles, commit themselves to resist cultural pressure toward conforming to affluent standards, and working toward societal changes to reduce hunger, poverty, injustice and structural violence. Unfortunately, this was true not only for the general public, but too often for Christians as well.

As we entered the year 1991, our nation faced a momentous decision whether we should vote to go to war or not to go to war. Six months earlier Iraq had invaded and now still occupied Kuwait. The United States and most nations agreed Iraq was wrong, and demanded them to leave Kuwait. With their continued refusal, our President asked Congress to authorize going to war. For the first time in our history, the leadership of most national church bodies opposed going to war at this time, and called for alternative efforts of negotiations or sanctions to resolve the matter. I was proud that American church leaders had boldly taken such a stand. On the Saturday before Congress was to vote on the War Decision, a hundred members of World Without War and other groups had gathered at our church to write and phone members of Congress urging them to vote 'no'. On Sunday, I urged people to write or phone their Congress representatives, expressing their opinion regarding the War Decision. However, I wanted them to know that I, as their pastor, believed Christian Peacemaking demanded a definite 'no' vote against going to war, and for continuing alternative efforts for resolving the conflict.

That day probably 80-90% of our congregation opposed going to war, although I heard the usual complaints from some that I was out of order to make such an announcement at worship services. The next day one of our members gave me a tape of the previous day's sermon from the pastor of a large nondenominational mega-church nearby, titled "When is it right for Christians to go to war?" and not surprisingly he said, "Now is such a time." Later that week Congress voted for the Gulf War, later called the First Gulf War. Within a month's time it was my opinion that the majority even in our congregation had changed their minds and approved that we had gone to war. In the nation undoubtedly the overwhelming majority approved.

I wondered at the power of our culture and the government's ability to manipulate public opinion. Even more I wondered how Christians could repudiate so easily the teaching and way of Jesus. And I wondered, how Christian leaders could so quickly become silent in the face of such a distortion of biblical and ethical imperatives.

For twenty centuries the church, within its own community, had faced division on various issues, both sides of the controversies defending themselves based on the life and teaching of Jesus and on scripture. I had been confronted with this situation constantly in my ministry, and it was now facing me again in the current controversy regarding the first Gulf War. Most of the pastors that I knew had privately voiced opposition to entering that war, but publicly had not said anything about it. Now they still opposed the war, yet they still remained publicly silent. Most voiced the opinion that "it is possible to support the soldiers without supporting their mission." However, I tried to make the case that if "supporting the soldiers" was the only thing people heard from their pastors regarding this war, people would assume their pastors also "supported this war and its mission." I often quoted Martin Luther King: "There comes a time when silence is betrayal."

The common view of church leaders seemed to be that pastors during conflict should have the goal of 'continuity of community', not 'agreement among its members'. The goal should be 'forgiving and accepting people', not 'like-mindedness'. They assumed that eventually differences on the issue of war and peace, as on other issues that continue among us, would be resolved finally with 'like-mindedness', but the reality for now must be accepted that disagreements on this issue would continue to exist. They argued that 'The Continuation of Our Community' and 'Our Life Together' requires the acceptance of differences and 'Unity amid Diversity' and 'Agreeing to Disagree' for the sake of 'Community' and for the 'Common Good'.

For me it was impossible to accept that conclusion regarding peace and justice issues. Even as slavery is wrong, and killing is wrong, and poverty is wrong when it can be prevented, so also violence is wrong and war is wrong when positive alternatives exist. Pastors were not only to comfort people, but were also to be prophetic witnesses to the ways of God as seen in the life and teachings of Jesus. The prophetic view is that Killing is wrong, and that War is presumed wrong. Reluctantly the Church had accepted the idea of a 'Justifiable War', and over the years had worked out the conditions necessary for war to be considered 'justifiable'. The Gulf War met none of those conditions. For me this was definitely a 'Kairos Moment', a time of critical importance, a time when truth must be faced, a moment of judgment, a moment of grace and opportunity, a time when God issues a challenge to make critical decisions and take decisive action. This concept of Kairos, which I had first encountered thirty years previously from Paul Tillich, was continually arising in my quest for peace. Without doubt, my personal Kairos was the depths and highs in my life—despair at the dropping of the Atomic bombs in August and then hope at the Peace Surrender Signings in September of 1945— the Marshall plan and then the Korean War—the Cold War and then Eisenhower's 'Warning— the Cuban/Russian/American Missile Crisis and then Kennedy's 'Quest for Peace— and now the opportunity for our nation and world to finally say 'No' and renounce War as an acceptable solution to conflict followed by the rejection of that opportunity by saying 'Yes' to the First Gulf War. As a nation, and as a church, we had faced a Kairos Moment, and had again failed the test.

Two years later, after nineteen rewarding years at this congregation, having served as a pastor for over forty years and reaching the age of sixty-seven, it was time for me to move on, and so I announced my retirement. On the last Saturday before my final Sunday, at a gala retirement celebration and banquet in our New Creation Center, our Bishop was invited to speak. In brief, his remarks touched me deeply and included:

> "In conclusion, First, you are a man that has not been out there just doing your own thing—but one who has invited us all to dance, in good times and tough times, both those who agreed with you and those that may have disagreed, an invitation to join in the dance. Second, you've also made us uncomfortable—but thanks for having the courage to do that. Third, you've always insisted that we look beyond ourselves, to more than being citizens of Orange County, or the U.S., but a part of God's great world around this globe—and not to forget the poor or the rich, the young or the old. There is only one thing that worries me when Jerry Pedersen retires; who is going to pick up the mantel, to have the courage to make mistakes, yes, but not be silent, and the courage to invite people to dance, that sometimes makes us very uncomfortable, and always calls us to look beyond ourselves. Thank you brother for a job well done."

As the evening retirement celebration was ending, my wife and I were blindfolded, and the several hundred guests quietly went outside. We were led out the door, and to my surprise as the blindfolds were taken off, surrounded by all the guests, was a new 4-door Ford Taurus with ribbons and balloons attached. They have continually reminded me, it was the first time they had ever seen me speechless! I was told that many people had personally donated to purchase the car, and that no church funds had been used. Dru and I accepted the gift as a true expression of their genuine love and appreciation for my having served them faithfully over the years, as well as having tolerated my many mistakes and, my many efforts badgering them forward on the social and justice issues that often made them uncomfortable.

The new car had special meaning for me as I remembered an earlier incident. We pastors had a reserved parking space for our cars near the office where I always parked my 25-year old VW bug in the space labeled 'Senior Pastor'. Its paint was faded and peeled, and the top especially rusted, resulting from having skidded off the road and rolling over on one of my forages near Oaxaca in southern Mexico. The top has been bashed in so far that I had to beat it out with a hammer just to make headroom to drive, which chipped off all the paint, causing the top to rust. One day two of our members had approached me in the church patio, and pointing to the car, told me that it just didn't look good for the church, that it was a disgrace to our large congregation having their senior pastor driving such a wreck of a car. They offered to arrange buying a new car for me if I would get rid of it. I politely said "no thanks", although I admit I was tempted. Privately, I gave them credit for being consistent— they were part of those who repeatedly objected to my 'political agenda', insisting many of my efforts were 'political', not 'biblical' or 'religious'. Fortunately, I also managed to be consistent trying to live 'The Way' as well as preach 'The Way'. Now, as I did receive the gift of a new car, I felt it was a truly a gift of love and appreciation for having been a friend and pastor living 'The Way'.

My retirement didn't really start that Saturday evening however, but rather the next day following our church services. My sermon that day was primarily reminiscences from the past, and challenging them to continue Walking The Way in the future. Though what I will never forget was when after the service had ended and I invited those who wanted to come gather around the table and share a final Eucharist together. Almost everyone came, and it was crowded

As I passed among them in the crowded confusion, I found I couldn't speak any words, but as I placed bread in the palm of their hand, I looked into the face and eyes of each person and recalled

*relationships that had been formed over the years... the teen who I
had baptized 17 years ago... the couple I had married... the housewife
who had walked the picket line supporting farm workers... the man
I had led to alcoholics anonymous... the mother of the son who had
committed murder... the abandoned child adopted by her new family...
the gay man who had found full acceptance in our midst... the widow
who just lost her husband ...the man I had visited in prison... the girl
who had been molested by her father... the woman who went to CCIDD
in Mexico with us and became a social activist...the woman who had
to forgive me for my insensitiveness to her situation... the sailor who
had trouble with the police... the conservative who disagreed with my
'politics' but thanked me for helping him understand other points of
view... the Jewish man who had told me he "didn't believe everything the
church teaches, but is a follower of the way of Jesus that we advocate"...
the man who says he comes every Sunday just to see what I'm going to
say that he disagrees with... the high school student who did his school
project interviewing me about conscientious objection... the man who
told me he didn't like for me to always be preaching about peace...
and his wife that did... the woman who helped organize and support
the food kitchen... the bridge partner who always bid too high... and
another who took too long in bidding... the man who claimed my
prayer with him in the hospital miraculously cured him... the woman
who discovered backpacking on our annual outing climbing San
Jack... the man who nearly left our church because I advocated the
ordination of gays and lesbians... and the man who came because I
did... the woman who went to Nicaragua with Witness for Peace... the
woman hurt by a divorce, but later found out it was really a blessing...
and... and... I could go on and on. It was an experience that will warm
my heart always! I had been truly blessed being accepted as a pastor,
and as a prophet, and as a friend.*

Later I often reflected on my over 40 years as a Pastor. I
remember some of the highs and lows of my experiences.

I remember the time at the Los Angeles County Hospital while
calling on a friend, when a nurse asked me to help a young Mexican
couple. The wife within the hour had just given premature birth
to a child that was now in an incubator. Going to the grieving
couple, with great difficulty understanding their language, I finally

understood they wished the baby baptized, naming it Juanita. Putting on hospital gown, mask, and rubber gloves, reaching through the opening in the incubator, placing my finger with a drop of water on the brow of the tiny baby hardly larger than my hand, I baptized the child. Doing so, and looking into the faces of the young couple and seeing smiles breaking out on their faces, against all hospital rules asked them to also put on gowns, masks, and rubber gloves and also reach in and gently touch Juanita's brow. After we had stepped outside the room and removed our gowns and masks, the nurse came out to tell me the child was now dead, and had probably been dead all this time. Feeling it best not to tell that to the couple, we joined hands and had a brief prayer, which they probably didn't understand, a prayer of thanksgiving for the love seen in this couple for their child. I then was able to find a Catholic priest at the hospital, and brought him to the couple to help comfort them in their own language. The priest and the couple thanked me profusely. Perhaps this was ecumenicity at its finest. Perhaps little of the words we had exchanged between us that day were understood, but I deeply felt satisfaction in ministering to that young couple, and undoubtedly this was one of my most rewarding pastoral moments.

I remember the time I baptized 85-year-old Ernest. Having worshipped with us several times, he approached me while leaving a service and said he want to be baptized. Suggesting that we meet later and arrange for his baptism, he said, "No, I want to be baptized now". And so we talked for an hour or so about his life, his faith, and his desire to be baptized 'now'. He said at 85 you don't put off things to another day. The only person around was the sexton who was busy arranging chairs, so he agreed to stand as a witness as I baptized Ernest. The joy on his face matched that of the young Mexican couple parents of Juanita, and I am sure the joy on my face matched the profound satisfaction in my heart.

I remember the times my sermons had received mixed reactions. Like my sermon statement that "as Christians we needed to accept the full inclusion of gay and lesbian persons in all we do, including accepting them for ordaining as clergy persons". One man, whom I had never met before, on the way out after the service as I greeted people at the door, grabbed my shoulders and shook me, angrily saying (actually, nearly yelling) that I was endorsing immorality and demanded I retract my statement. I asked him to wait a few minutes and I would be glad to discuss this with him, but he angrily went away, and I never saw him again. Then, one of the last people to leave asked me to see him the next day. When we met, he acknowledged he was gay and had lapsed from the church for many years because the church in which he was raised had rejected him. He said he had come to this church because he had heard we were different. And with tears in his eyes, he thanked me for my sermon, and soon became an active participant in the congregation.

I remember the time on Christmas Eve two days after returning from two weeks with Witness for Peace on the Nicaraguan-Honduras border acting as a peacemaker between Contra and Sandinista forces. In the sermon I mentioned that we ought not only recall the Christmas story of 'Joy to the World' and 'Peace to all' of Christ's birth, but also the continuing story of 'Herod's Killing of the Innocent Children' that followed it. And then I mentioned that the same was happening in our day, and gave as example the struggle for the 'good news' of freedom in Nicaragua which I had witnessed only days before, yet also the 'bad news' that our country was supporting efforts trying to suppress and destroy that freedom. Several persons following the service complained that I had no right to inject 'politics' into the Christmas Eve celebration and that they were going to demand I stop speaking 'politics from the pulpit'. I tried to suggest we have some follow-up studies of the place of politics in religious life, or the relationship between church and state, but they took off grumbling. We did follow up with such forums, but the complainers didn't participate.

I remember that I had always tried to live my common daily life sacramentally, that is, as sensing the sacred in the midst of the so-called profane. Celebrating the Sacraments had never really been my highest priority. However, some of my most memorable memories were of sharing Holy Communion. Like the time sharing the Eucharist while kneeling in the dust out in the open grape fields during the United Farm Workers strike, with hundreds of farm workers and their families together with Cesar Chavez, and hearing

Chavez talk of the necessity of keeping all their actions nonviolent as essential to winning public support for the justice of their cause. Neither would the students that came with me from San Francisco State University forget his words when we returned to the campus, and months later themselves involved in their Student Strike, and their efforts to do it nonviolently. In their own student strike they were to see how a few students failing to act nonviolently helped to discredit the Strike in the public's eye, even though administration and government intruders, and not students, had initiated most of the violence. They also would learn that basic structural violence perpetuating unjust practices in university education and its resistance to change was the real culprit. Now, kneeling in the dust alongside Robert Kennedy and field workers and students, only months before Kennedy's run for President in 1968, an election he probably would have won had he not been assassinated, and receiving bread and dipping it in the wine from surrounding grape fields was for me a deeply sacramental moment, a moment I would remember every time in the future I shared Holy Communion with a community, as well as remembering Jesus sharing it 2000 years ago with his community.

I remember the many times we celebrated Communion using the suggestion of my good friend John Arthur called the Lord's Meal, especially at weekend retreats. Done during a regular meal at lunch or dinner, conversation would be encouraged among the group commenting on where they might have seen the Spirit of God working in events reported in the daily paper that day or in their work experiences that week or perhaps in event in their lives. Interspersed with the discussion, especially as a situation seemed to reveal a spiritual depth or a new hope, or maybe even in a desperate situation like a possible war breaking out or an election or a surgery to be performed, bread would be shared, or all would be asked to drink of their wine, or a cup of wine would be passed for each to drink from as we celebrated God's gifts of life, food, friendship, and the Spirit's Presence. I especially remember the time sharing the crisis I went thru while overseas upon hearing of the dropping of the atomic bomb, wondering about the loss of our humanity, and asking where was God in this? Others recalled similar experiences in their military service, especially two younger men who had recently served in Vietnam. Interestingly, one said God was never so near to him as when he was in the midst of battle. The other said he stopped believing in God altogether in his time there, that the suffering and death and violence, not only of the Vietnamese villagers, but among his fellow war-mates as well, including corruption, immorality and acts of inhumanity that made believing in a God impossible for him. The discussion following went on so long that the afternoon agenda had to be set back over an hour. The discussion made meaningful that in remembering Jesus in this Lord's Meal we were also remembering that he was no stranger to this kind of suffering and death, remembering also the sharing of forgiveness among ourselves and with God, and remembering the gift of new life and hope and resurrection. People have often asked "Do you suppose this is the way the first Lord's Supper really happened" and I would usually say "Perhaps something like that." When people have made comments like "Every meal should be like that, even at home or at church," I've said that realistically I don't think that is always possible, and yet every meal and every worship or liturgy experience has that Sacramental possibility of a common experience conveying an eternal Spiritual Awareness or a God Consciousness or Presence of Christ, call it what you will.

The years following my retirement until the dawn of the new millennium were filled with many rewarding experiences. I had the opportunity to supply short-term interim pastoral leadership in several congregations, usually in troubling situations. Locally, in the midst of harassment by hate groups toward both Muslims and Jews by red-neck Americans due to the pressures resulting from Israeli/Palestinian conflict and other issues, we were able to help provide better understanding and relationships by efforts of our Interfaith Peace Ministry in Orange County. Nationally, I served on the Board of Lutheran Peace Fellowship and as its Chairman, and with the guidance of Glen Gersmehl as its Coordinator, we were able bring leaders from all parts of the nation to Texas for Active Nonviolence Training, promote special peace training especially among youth, and promote other peace and justice efforts. Another rewarding opportunity was returning twice to Holden Village, a unique retreat center in the remote high mountain country of central Washington, where I was able to spend several weeks offering small group classes or discussion groups on Forgiveness, Reconciliation, Friendship, and Nonviolence. More than thirty years earlier, in 1963 or 1964, as a Campus Pastor at Portland State University, I had taken a group of students to the newly formed Holden Village to help rebuild the former mining camp as a retreat center. And the last year before the new millennium I had the privilege to serve one year as an interim Campus Pastor at Stanford University upon the recommendation of a good friend and fellow activist Campus Pastor Herb Schmidt, upon his retirement after his long and successful tenure there. It was a rare opportunity to compare prestigious private Stanford University with the State Universities I had served in San Francisco and Portland, Oregon and the overseas Universities in Tanzania, Africa and London, England. I found that each had its own strengths and weaknesses, advantages and disadvantages, even as I had discovered in my experiences as a student at the multi and diverse colleges and universities and seminaries and graduate schools that I had attended.

Now I was to continue my Unfinished Journey as I anticipated in a New Century, a century that Martin Luther King said would be one of either "Nonviolence or Nonexistence." I was filled with a powerfully felt hope that the peoples of the earth had learned from bitter experience that there was a better way for living than most had known in the last century. And I was convinced that there was a better way, the way of peace. And surely we had learned, there is no way to peace, peace is the way!

PART III:
THE JOURNEY—AN UNFINISHED JOURNEY

Every gun that is made, every warship launched, every rocket fired, signifies in the final sense a theft from those who hunger and are not fed, those who are cold and are not clothed. This world in arms is not spending money alone. It is spending the sweat of its laborers, the genius of its scientists, the hopes of its children.

—President Dwight D. Eisenhower

Chapter 8

JANUARY 1, 2000: A New Beginning

I HAD HIGH HOPES for a new beginning for human history, as we were to enter the new century, the dawn of the third millennium. The Lutheran Peace Fellowship and Holden Village together hosted 'Peace is the Way,' a very special retreat on nonviolence over the New Year's holiday. For several days we shared our ideas and hopes about nonviolent peacemaking, and ended with the opportunity to take the vow of nonviolence. It was our way of preparing to live 'The Year for the Culture of Peace' proclaimed for the year 2000 by the United Nations General Assembly, and to live the 'International Decade for a Culture of Peace and Nonviolence for the Children of the World' proclaimed for the decade 2001-2010. Having made that nonviolent vow in the last hours of the ending century, and now standing outdoors in the first hours of the new century in a new millennium, with the moonlight reflecting on the several feet of snow covering the ground and the snow laden trees, and feeling awed by the mountain peaks jutting up around us thousands of feet, I offered a prayer that our dreams and hopes might be fulfilled for a world of peace.

No one was more excited about the new millennium coming than I was. It definitely was a time people expected new beginnings. For me, I felt that maybe, just maybe, humanity would have benefited from the lessons learned from the past, and be ready to enter the new millennium determined to create a better world, especially ready to begin settling international conflicts through negotiation and good will, rather than through the violence of war and killing.

As a child I remember being confident that I would live to be 100 years old, in good health, and welcoming the year 2000 as I began the last quarter of my life. Then I studied hard and made the scholarship group all through school and earned my Eagle Scout badge in Scouting. Then, immediately 8 days following my high school graduation in 1943 during the second World War, I began active duty in the U.S. Marine Corps, hoping to help bring 'peace to the world'.

That is where my journey for peacemaking began, and now I had come to that point when time moved from one millennium to enter another. In this new millennium I was determined to try to do as the Jewish Talmud says, "doing justly, now; loving mercy, now; walking humbly, now", and adding as someone has said "and though I am not obligated to complete the work, neither am I free to abandon it." And I, as a Christian, chose to seek the way of peace in this new millennium, not from the point-of-view of some mushy sentiment, but from hardheaded common sense.

After 75 years on this journey of peacemaking, I knew the task would not be easy in this new millennium. Bitter experience prepared me to know that it is far easier to decry what doesn't work than to envision and bring about the positive alternatives that would make for a more peaceful world.

As the New Year came and the new millennium started, the media had predicted major catastrophic happenings. Some said that since computers were primed to '19' rather than '20', the turn of the century would result in major disruptions in all areas of life. Others predicted the 'second-coming' or 'Armageddon' or 'the rapture' would happen. The fact that the date had been determined during the sixth century and devised by the method of counting years from the purported birth of Jesus Christ made it a rather arbitrary date used in western culture. Jews use a different method for counting time, and Muslims count from Muhammad's flight to Medina in 622 AD. And other people, of other cultures and with differing religions, do not necessarily recognize this as the beginning of a new millennium. So it was no surprise that nothing unusual happened as our calendars turned to 2000, or to 2001 as some argued to be the accurate date for beginning the new millennium

Two crucial issues gained my attention as we began the new millennium. I felt how we handled these two issues would determine whether the new century would bring destruction and regression, or progress toward hope and a more peaceful world. The first of these issues was whether the new century would be one of violent conflict or nonviolent conflict. The second was whether the new century would succeed or fail in lifting the massive poverty throughout the world. I was hopeful, even optimistic, for a positive resolution of both issues, that it would be 'The Nonviolent Century' of humankind having learned to settle conflicts peacefully, and 'The Century of Overcoming Poverty'.

Regarding the first issue, looking backward, the twentieth century would be remembered as the 'Century of Violence', the most violent century in history, violence having been inflicted on a scale never before seen, or even possible. Twentieth century history could be written as holocaust, ethnic cleansing, genocide, arms race, revolution, totalitarianism, exploitation or warfare

Russia alone lost nearly thirty million dead in the two world wars. The Nazi's Holocaust killed over 5 million people, Dresden was nearly destroyed in one night's bombings, two atomic bombs destroyed two Japanese cities, and firebombs killed a million in other cities. The violence of warfare took over 70 million lives in Europe between 1914 and 1945, and the scope of violence kept increasing, from the trench warfare in WWI, to the saturation bombing of WWII, to atomic bombs at Hiroshima, to a thermonuclear arms race leading to MAD (Mutually Assured Deterrence) and the threat of total destruction. Killings increased from hundreds to thousands to millions, and increased from the killing of primarily military personnel to the incidental collateral damage of killing even larger numbers of civilians. Somehow, we had moved from thinking that killing one person is murder, to killing ten persons is monstrous, to honoring those killing thousands of people as being heroic.

The 'Mother in Wartime' poem that Langston Hughes wrote after WWII— "She thought that one side won, not that both might lose "—really described the mistaken belief in 'Redemptive Violence' that controlled our thinking, that *'our'* use of justifiable violence would somehow be redeeming, bringing justice, and even peace, in response to *'their'* unjustifiable use of violence.

In the 55 years following the end of WWII until the end of the century, the U.S. engaged in bombing 20 different countries, supposedly to correct the evils of their undemocratic governments. Yet, not in any of these instances did a democratic government, respectful of human rights, occur as a direct result. A lesson that we ought to have learned during the last century is that the promise of war to stamp out evil is mistaken. Reality is that war itself is the evil. Evil begets evil. Violence begets violence. Peace doesn't just happen when evil is eradicated, especially when evil is used to eradicate it. Peace isn't the absence of war. Peace doesn't spontaneously spring up when war ends. Peace is not simply a tranquil static lifeless condition. Peace is like life itself, like any growing organism. It has to be grown, planted, nurtured, cultivated and cared for. We should have learned that the promise of war to bring peace is a lie.

The violence of the Twentieth Century for us in America was made possible in part because of the steady stream of dishonesty from those in power. The century began with our being told the lie that our reason for invading Cuba was in response to our enemies sinking our battleship in their Cuban harbor. Justification for entry into WWI was supposedly to make the world safe for democracy, however proved to be far more about advancing imperial powers. Eisenhower and Kennedy lied about our growing involvement in Vietnam, and Johnson continued with the lie about the Gulf of Tonkin incident, and Nixon continued with lying about extending the bombing into Cambodia. Invading Grenada and Panama surely were not because they were a threat to us. And the first Iraq War was about our interest in Middle East oil, not our concern for poor little Kuwait. If our leaders had been honest, we would have acknowledged that our concern was less to 'stop communism' or 'protect democracy', and more to protect our so-called 'national interest', which was not the interest of 'we the people', but of large corporations and 'money interests'. Lying and violence became as American as apple pie.

All these are examples of 'Hot' types of violence' that receive vast media attention. However, the 'Cold' types of violence', such as the estimated thirty to forty thousand daily preventable deaths of children from hunger, receive very little media attention. This cold type of violence is 'Structural Violence', or 'Institutional Violence', or 'Violence of the Status Quo', and is increasingly prevalent in America. And it is the way things now work in our society, and it perpetually works against the interests of many of it's citizens. In San Francisco, for example, it was easy for me to see the violence of the slum—not just the 'acts' of violence 'in' the slum, but the violence 'of' the slum itself—the environment and structure which harms those who live and grow up within it. Those living in the slums may never be mugged or raped, and yet the inferior schools they attend, the health care they don't receive, and the lack of good job opportunities for themselves and for their children are the realities of 'structural violence'. Again, during the height of the Vietnam War, twice as many black people than white people were drafted proportionate to their numbers in the U.S. and sent to war, even though Selective Service was supposed to have been designed to avoid such inequities. Structural Violence has been a reality probably since time began, but population growth, the movement from farms to cities, the growth of the technological society and other factors during the last century had contributed to its being the Century of Violence.

As the century drew to a close, one of my heroes was Dan Berrigan, who talked about half-hearted peacemakers, who talk of peace, yet are unwilling to pay any significant price for it. Berrigan said: "Because we want peace with half a heart and half a life and will, wars continue, because the waging of war, by its nature, is total—while the waging of peace, by our cowardice, is partial." His own life, and his challenge to us, is to devote the same discipline and self-sacrifice to nonviolent peacemaking that armies devote to war.

Fortunately, the last century was not only a violent one. It had also witnessed the growing influence and impact of a Century of Active Nonviolence all over the world.

149

I had personally participated in one of these experiences during the 1980s when I traveled to Nicaragua with 'Witness for Peace'. As part of a team of ten people from the U.S., following several days of nonviolence training, I had spent two weeks there in a small village near the village of Esteli, close to the Honduras border, where the Contra forces from Honduras were fighting and killing local people who supported the Sandinista government of Nicaragua. Hardly a day passed that we didn't hear gunfire and see evidence of fighting and killings. However, since our presence as U.S. citizens had been widely publicized and broadcast over the radio, and since the Contras wanted to avoid the negative effect of having killed or injured Americans, we were told that local fighting and killing was considerably lessened after we arrived. Later we were to learn that over seven years, with hundreds of 'Witness for Peace' volunteers visiting villages along the border, not one Nicaraguan village was ever attacked by the contras while Witness for Peace volunteers were present. We had been instructed to be seen widely in public and on the streets, and assigned to sleep in small houses scattered throughout the village and surrounding area. My assigned *'casa'* was very small, having one bedroom where the parents slept with their three children, resulting in me sleeping in a hammock outside in the yard with chickens and pigs wandering around underneath, and awakening to the smell of fresh tortillas and beans being prepared on the outside wood burning fireplace for breakfast. During the day we would share in working in the fields, or helping in a children's center, or talking to local community leaders or militias or women's groups and conducting nonviolence training.

This experience, together with my experiences in Africa and the Civil Rights movements during the 1960s, together with my experiences in Central and South America with 'Liberation Theology', 'Small Based Christian Communities', and the 'Cuernavaca Center for Intercultural Dialogue on Development', convinced me of the importance of large groups of people in organized peaceful nonviolent actions that inspire hope and call people to higher values. I was excited to go to Nicaragua to support the hopeful change that the revolution had brought to their country in 1979. After 50 years of the long struggle of the Nicaraguan people to free themselves from foreign domination, they had been finally able to oust the brutal and corrupt U.S. installed Somoza dictatorship. When I was younger I had been taught in my schooling that our 'Monroe Doctrine' policies guaranteed freedom from foreign intervention for all of America, but had come to realize that it really meant only that we were determined to keep out all other nations so that we could control the rest of the Americas for our own benefit. This had been truthfully acknowledged by former president Franklin Roosevelt when he spoke of the corrupt Somoza: "He may be a son of a bitch, but he's our son of a bitch." I became convinced that the Sandinista Government that the U.S. was opposing, while it may not have been perfect, was at least the government that represented and fought for the interests of the people of Nicaragua and not for the ruling rich. However, for a variety of reasons, not the least of which was the powerful opposition of our own government, the Sandinista Revolution finally failed in achieving the lofty goals it had set out to achieve, as had most efforts during the century in the Americas south of us. Fortunately, these failures were not the case in many places all over the world during the last century.

As violent as the 20th Century had been, there are many people who believe as I do that the 20th Century will be finally remembered for something other than its violence. It will be remembered as the century when a powerful alternative to violence will have been discovered and put into practice in overcoming injustice and violence. The alternative—'nonviolence', or even better, 'active nonviolence', or 'nonviolent direct action'—was to become a most powerful force exploding in amazing and unexpected ways in a century of conflict. Someone has said that the understanding and practice of nonviolence at the beginning of the 20th Century was akin to the primitive understanding about electricity prior to Edison's time. However beginning with Mahatma Gandhi and further developed and practiced by M.L. King and Cesar Chavez and others during the century, what had previously been know as 'pacifism' became a powerful force for social and political change. No longer was it merely a passive, neutral and largely individual private idea, but had become a powerful and vigorous direct action social movement practiced by large groups of people.

Although the idea of nonviolence had been advocated in many cultures and by most religions for centuries, in the last century it was Mohandas Gandhi who was the first to practice it as a strategy for bringing about massive social change. His philosophy was rooted in Hindu and Indian traditions, inspired by the life of Jesus, and first practiced in South Africa in the early part of the last century. By refusing to obey unjust laws that required registration by Indians in South Africa, without resorting to violence, and accepting the consequences, he was able to change the minds of his oppressors and change those laws.

Returning to India, he led a movement practicing nonviolent direct action against British rule, finally defeating what was then the mightiest empire on earth and gaining India's independence. He was able to demonstrate by nonviolent action that governments are dependent on the consent of the people they govern. When the people followed his strategy of not paying unjust taxes, of not obeying unjust laws, and of noncooperation, he was able to demonstrate that active nonviolent 'people power' could accomplish what violent power could not. Gandhi believed that nonviolent resistance, or *'Satyagraha'* (truth force) as he called it, was the 'mightiest force in the world', which operated much like the laws of science, and if consistently practiced, it would be a mighty power for bringing a more just society.

The book *'A Force More Powerful'* and its PBS documentary describes the nonviolent process Gandhi used to bring about these changes in India. The book then goes on to describe some of the nonviolent social movements that followed, including the Civil Rights Movement in America led by King, the movement to overcome 'Apartheid' and leading to independence in South Africa, resisting the Nazis by Danes, opposing communism by Poles, resisting dictators by Chileans and Filipinos, and bringing increased justice and peace to those lands. Strikes and boycotts, demonstrations and noncooperation, civil disobedience and sit-ins were used to topple tyrannical governments, oppose occupying armies, and bring about civil and human rights that had been denied masses of people. The prevailing view had been that relying on a *'redemptive violence'* was the ultimate power for maintaining the status quo, or alternatively for overthrowing it to gain a just cause or to defeat injustice. However, this use of violence always brought more violence, and injustices continued in different forms. During the past century the effectiveness of wisely used *'nonviolent direct action'* was shown as able to bring down ruthless governments or military powers and to establish justice. As Cesar Chavez had said to us earlier: "We are only just beginning to understand the power of love because we are just beginning to understand the weakness of force and oppression."

Yes, we are only just beginning to understand the power of love expressed through active nonviolence, but we have begun! Not only the described 'Witness for Peace' and *'A Force More Powerful',* but many other ordinary people movements throughout the world and working against all kinds of oppression and violence have successfully renounced the use of violence and demonstrated the effectiveness of nonviolent action to bring positive change. Dozens of other nongovernmental organizations devoted to nonviolent intervention are at work, including 'Peaceworkers', 'Peace Brigades International', 'Christian Peacemaker Teams', and the 'Global Nonviolent Peace Force' (GNPF), to name just a few. The GNPF proposes to develop an international, multiethnic standing peace force that will be trained in nonviolent strategies and tactics and deployed to conflicts or potentially violent areas. Humanitarian intervention in such conflict situations to stop violence is desperately needed, since most governments, and even the United Nations, deploy armed troops, supposedly to keep the peace, but armed soldiers with guns all too often only succeed in fanning the flames of violence. Therefore, nonpartisan civilian peace teams trained in pacifist strategies are more likely to be received than are soldiers with guns. Gandhi was actually working on such a *Shanti Sena* (Peace Army) when he was assassinated. Not only is such an approach morally desirable, it is pragmatically more effective and less costly. The proposal to begin this GNPF in the new millennium estimates that it is likely to cost $80 million a year to begin an operation of a Peace Army of 2,000 active participants, and while this seems a lot of money, the world spends more than this on military operations each and every hour of every day of the year, and nearly half of it is being spent by the United States. M.L. King said: "World peace through nonviolent means is neither absurd nor unattainable. All other methods have failed. Thus we must begin anew." The recent history of nonviolent methods to bring about positive justice and peaceful changes in our world were not chosen only for principled reasons, or even to avoid the spilling of blood. They were often chosen for pragmatic reasons, perhaps because they had no other options, or perhaps simply because they felt nonviolent actions would have a better chance of being successful.

My hopes for a Peaceful millennium were heightened when the United Nations General Assembly responded to an appeal from every living Nobel Peace Laureate by proclaiming the year 2000 to be 'The Year for the Culture of Peace' and the years 2001-2010 to be the 'International Decade for a Culture of Peace and Nonviolence for the Children of the World'. To fulfill that hope, it was essential to recognize the violence surrounding us, recognizing that we live in a culture of violence as evidenced by the fact that one out of every five U.S. children lives in poverty while we spend billions upgrading our nuclear arsenal, and that the majority of our aid to foreign countries takes the form of military weapons. Therefore, although I had several times previously been trained for specific nonviolent direct actions at civil rights demonstrations and peace protests such as at the Nevada Nuclear Test Site, I now chose to enlist in a more thorough nonviolence training with 'Pace e Bene Franciscan Nonviolence Center'. Then with 'Lutheran Peace Fellowship' I helped train others as nonviolence activists using the Pace e Pene's 'From Violence to Wholeness' training manual. One of my most rewarding experiences was leading a group of twenty high school students from 12 different congregations, using a version of the manual 'From Violence to Wholeness' that I had adapted for youth, and then seeing several of them utilize their training in High School activities. Since being retired I had more time than previously to organize and train others in the practice and benefits of nonviolence, and helping them to embrace the nonviolent way of Jesus and becoming voices of hope and light, especially for children, and for the world.

As the new century began, I remembered the words of someone who had suggested that at the beginning of the last century people's knowledge about how nonviolence worked was comparable to the primitive knowledge of electricity prior to Edison's time. They did have the living examples of nonviolence as practiced at the 'personal' level in the lives of Jesus, St. Francis, Tolstoy and others, but even as Chavez had reminded us; well into the last century we had only begun understanding the power of nonviolence. However, a growing number of people were becoming convinced of the weakness of violence, even though most people, as Dan Berrigan had reminded us, were still only halfheartedly working for peace while totally waging war. During the first half of the last century Gandhi had demonstrated that nonviolence was 'the most powerful force in the world' not only at the 'personal' level, but at the 'social' public level as well. Then King had shared his 'dream' and demonstrated by 'direct nonviolent action' steps toward its realization. Finally, in the latter part of the century groups and organizations throughout the world had demonstrated that renouncing 'militaristic violent actions', which were incapable of achieving justice and peace, and opting instead for the more effective 'nonviolent direct action', they could achieve powerful changes for justice and peace. It was this realization that gave me hope as we entered the new century.

My second major hope for the New Year was a serious reduction of poverty throughout the world, and of course that hope is closely related to my first hope, the elimination of violence. I was excited that, after much preparation prior to 2000, the recommendation of the United Nations, The Millennium Development Goals (MDG), had been adopted by 189 nations with a sense of urgency. It established eight goals to be achieved by 2015, goals that "respond to the world's main development challenges to share the benefits of globalization more fairly." The first goal, eradication of extreme poverty, aimed to " free our fellow men, women, and children from the abject and dehumanizing conditions of extreme poverty, to which more than a billion of them are currently subjected." The other seven goals, each important on its own, were important for fulfillment of the first poverty goal. These seven goals included achieving universal primary education, promoting gender equality and empowering women, reducing child mortality, improving maternal health, combating HIV/AIDS and other diseases, ensuring environmental sustainability, and developing global partnership for development.

However, my excitement over the adoption of the MDG was mitigated by my distrust of *'development'* based on values and models of the rich or powerful, and on the structures of injustice devised by the rich to preserve and enhance their privileges. Even though the MDG are to be carefully monitored and evaluated every five years to ensure that they are being carried out as planned, experience has been that *'liberation'*, not *'development'*, is needed. The poor must be enabled to use their energies to work for their own welfare. Recognizing that since those in power do not willingly give up their privileges, the poor themselves must no longer see themselves as victims who have no power, and assert their resistance to the prevailing power structures, which is within their power. History has shown that although a few *'individuals'* of the rich may willingly take the initiative to surrender power and control, as a *'class'* they don't. And a few *'individuals'* of the poor may have succeeded in the past to climbing out of poverty, but as a *'class'* they haven't. History has also shown that 'people power' expressed as *militant violence* only continues or increases violence or injustice in other forms, whereas 'people power' expressed as well organized and disciplined *nonviolent direct action* during the last century was able to bring significant social change for justice. Only this concept of *'liberation'* together with the MDG offers hope for achieving these goals.

In our day TV and other media have so inundated us with pictures and statistics of poverty around the world that many of us have come to accept it as an unfortunate yet unalterable state of affairs. Regrettably, many of those living in poverty have also internalized this, seeing themselves as hopeless victims over which they have no control. But it is not only the poor who see poverty as inevitable. The idea that poverty is inevitable is part of the mythology of our culture. Since poverty is assumed to be the fate of humanity and there is no hope for ending it, the myth contributes to sustaining unjust dominant political and economic structures in America.

Much of my life has been spent with university and church people who have had limited experiences with hunger and poverty, and even these few experiences have often been with people with symptoms of social dysfunction. Such experiences have led them to an individualistic understanding of poverty, with poverty often being seen primarily as due to some personal moral failure. High school and college courses, and some church instruction, can assist young people and other adults to a broader view of understanding poverty resulting from the structured injustice found in economic and social systems. However, I have found much of this formal education, whether secular or religious, to be of limited value, in itself rarely changing people's attitudes and behavior for social change. For people who value Scripture, introducing them to the prophets of the Old Testament helps them understand that these prophets are less concerned about predicting the future than they are about the immediate impact of societal evils that are creating poverty and hunger. As such, these prophets are not predictors of the future, but rather, social analysts calling for social change. Understanding this view of Scripture, they can then go on to examine contemporary forms of societal and institutional injustice that produce poverty and hunger. When this is combined with actual experiences of disciplined guided exposure to conditions of domestic or foreign poverty, together with training in nonviolent direct action and opportunities for service with nonviolent social movements, dramatic commitments to positive social changes occur.

I am constantly reminded of a comment made to me by a friend, an economics professor who called himself an 'anarchist Marxist Christian', who said: "we Christians are lucky to have poor people around so we can occasionally give them a food basket, which doesn't really solve their problems but helps us salve our consciences, tweak our egos, and makes us feel better." It's true. The problems of poverty remain, and charity itself does nothing to solve them, and perhaps even encourages its perpetuation, regardless of our good intentions of helping. Living in East Africa I often felt as my friend did as I observed Muslims doing their 'religious duty' dropping small coins into cans held by the many beggars on the street. Compassion is at the heart of all true religion, and charity is rightly encouraged by all religion, however unless achieving justice is given the highest priority of compassion, charity can be counter-productive. It can help provide the safety net every society needs, in the same way that governmental public assistance does, but neither is a substitute for seeking a more equitable inclusive just society. Charity as a temporary and stopgap necessity is undoubtedly needed, although advocating for better education, health care, job training, full employment, better housing and other justice requirements for everyone so that everyone has a place at the table must be our constant endeavor and the goal we're trying to reach.

Technological advances, globalization, and new political realities have created dramatic changes in recent years, encouraging new opportunities to improve economies and reduce hunger. The 'Millennium Development Goals' must be 'Minimum' Goals. Anything less would be morally unacceptable. When we consider the billions of dollars for conducting wars that is 'spent'—'wasted' would be a more accurate word, or even more so, 'robbed' from all people and especially the poor—the much smaller amount of money and resources needed to alleviate poverty is relatively small change. President Eisenhower was clearly right in his final presidential address when he warned us of the dangers of excessive military spending that robs from the hungry, unfed and poor. We have been guilty of that, and have been the world's biggest offender by far.

As we entered the new millennium I was truly hopeful, even optimistic, that we were well on the way to a more peaceful future, the kind of peace that makes possible a better life for all people everywhere, that settles conflicts nonviolently, including those that lead to war, and reduces poverty, at home and abroad. All nations through the United Nations had set out in the first decade of the new century to create a Culture of Peace and Nonviolence, and had set Millennium Development Goals that aimed to eliminate poverty and ensure the conditions making the Decade Goals possible. I wondered if it could be possible that perhaps Jesus' vision and call to "love God and neighbor and even our enemy" had now actually become the accepted agenda of all humanity? Perhaps Gandhi's demonstration that Satyagraha (truth-force) could work in South Africa and India among masses of people to bring justice to a social situation was catching on all over the world. Perhaps King's demonstration of Direct Nonviolent Action for creating advancement of human rights in America actually was an effective way to achieve them whereas other approaches had failed. Perhaps Chavez's insistence that poor uneducated but trained disciplined field workers practicing nonviolence could bring about more just working conditions in the grape fields of California had demonstrated the best hope for fulfilling the Decade of Nonviolence. Perhaps the numerous Nonviolent Social Movements that had achieved positive social changes in many areas of the world during the latter part of the last century had shown that "there is no way to peace, peace is the way", that Jesus' 'Love' and Gandhi's 'Satyagraha' and King's 'Nonviolence' were in fact 'A Force More Powerful' that would make possible my hopes for this new century.

"One day we must come to see that peace is not merely a distant goal that we seek, but that it is a means by which we arrive at the goal. We must pursue peaceful ends through peaceful means."

—*Martin Luther King*

Chapter 9

SEPTEMBER 11, 2001: An Awakening

THE MORNING OF SEPTEMBER 11, 2001, along with millions of others, I watched on TV the airplane that smashed into the World Trade Center (WTC), and the smoke that bellowed out of the hole and windows of the building before suddenly collapsing to the ground. As I watched, I remembered and pictured in my mind images of Pearl Harbor on December 7, 1941—of planes and bombs and smoke rising from battleships at Pearl Harbor, and images of Hiroshima on August 6, 1945—of the cloud that arose after the Atom bomb exploded above Hiroshima. Now, as I watched the events of 9/11/01, I remembered that back then at those earlier moments in 1941 and 1945, I really hadn't fully comprehended the meaning of what was taking place before my eyes. That meaning required a better understanding of the history of the years that had preceded them. For me, that understanding only began on August 6,1945, that day out in the Pacific Ocean as I heard that 'we', America, had dropped an Atomic Bomb that destroyed an entire city, killing thousands of people—only began as I felt the ambiguity of both elation because the war was nearing its end and the shame that 'we', America, would drop such a bomb. Yet at those moments it was not only the causes of the violence of those earlier days that I didn't understand, but also the results of continuing violence from those days. It had taken me a long time to learn the truth spoken by A.J. Muste, "There is no way to peace, peace is the way", or by M.L. King, "Violence can't overcome darkness, only light can do that", or

161

by Cesar Chavez, "We're only beginning to understand the power of nonviolence as we're learning the weakness of force"

That morning of 9/11/01 I also remember sharing for a moment with others the urge for revenge, for wanting to strike back and destroy those who did it. And for a moment I too asked "Why did this happen?" and "Why do they hate us?" However, remembering the nearly 60 years I had been on my Unfinished Journey questing for peace, I soon began to partially understand why they hate us. Then when I heard others asking "Why would 'they' attack the WTC, symbol of the power and might of 'our' America, especially after 'all that we have done for them'?" I realized that my dreams and hopes for the new millennium had to face the reality of real life and the continuing darkness of day

Therefore, as part of a collective effort by the Lutheran Peace Fellowship for a statement on how we should respond, I immediately put my thoughts down on paper of how we should respond to the attack on the WTC. Rejecting my initial feelings of anger and need for revenge and retribution toward those who had conducted those attacks, I sent the following to our coordinator.

> "Any response against violence and terrorism must recognize that we too (as private citizens and collectively as American citizens) live in a culture of violence, and typically respond to violence with counter-violence. As Christians, committed to the Way of Jesus, and Gandhi and King, the Way of Active Nonviolence, in addition to seeking to find those responsible for the attacks and bringing them to justice, our response as people and as a nation should include the following: 1) We must begin seriously addressing the United Nations' call for creating the Decade of Nonviolence; 2) We must seriously begin addressing the personal violence that resides too much in each of us; 3) We must seriously begin recognizing America's complicity in supporting, among other things, the unjust violence of Israeli policy toward Palestinians, the violence to civilians and especially children in our boycott of Iraq, our national prioritizing of militarism above elimination of

poverty at home and abroad, and changing our refusal to effect the full cancellation of the debt of the most impoverished nations of the world (which according to UN figures) accounts for the death of 19,000 children a day in countries in the Southern Hemisphere (this last item a suggestion of good friend Bill Lesher); and 4) Refrain from demonizing Islam in these bombings, since radical Islamic groups like the Taliban are to Islam even as hawkish Israeli groups are to Judaism or white supremacist groups are to Christianity. We must make it clear that the LPF believes that only by actively pursuing nonviolence can we begin overcoming violence in our world."

The following morning, September 12th, I was proud of my pastor Scot Sorensen when he delivered the following prayer on the floor of the California State Assembly that in part read:

"O Lord God, You teach us to love our enemies and pray for those who hate us, but those seem so far from our imagination. On our own, Lord, we don't know how to love our enemies. On our own, we might seek vengeance and revenge. But vengeance is not justice, and revenge will not put out the fires of anger within us. Lord, more than ever, we need you. We need you to touch us with your grace, to fill us with your compassion, and to remind us that we are all, all of us, are your precious children."

We didn't have to wait long for President Bush to inform us of why he thought they hated us and attacked the WTC. "Osama bin Laden is an evil man", and "this is a struggle between good and evil". It is as simple as that. Americans are fundamentally good and compassionate, and terrorists are fundamentally bad. And within days we were to hear from bin Laden on TV, saying the "winds of change have come". "What America is tasting now is something insignificant compared to what we have tasted for scores of years. May God show them His wrath and give them what they deserve." He refers then to Japan and our dropping the Atomic bomb as a war crime that we still justify, and on our hateful policies toward the Islamic world. Then he says "these events have divided the whole world into two sides—the side of believers and the side of infidels—neither America nor the people who live in it will dream of security before we live it in Palestine, and not before all the infidel armies leave the land of Mohammad."

Both the President and bin Laden offered simple explanations of the problem, and also offered simple solutions. It was the same speech given by both, only the names had changed, each one mirroring reflections of the other. I too wish there was a simple solution and simple answers, but we should all know there are no simplistic solutions. Although we cannot determine how others will react, we do have the choice of our own actions. While it is true that we must do what we can to stop others from attacking us, we must do it without sacrificing our own moral values. Revenge and retribution is the action of terrorists; it must not be ours, deepening the downward spiral of violence. Using the term 'evil' is probably the most morally condemning and judgmental word about another human that we can use. It dangerously cuts off any possibility of communication or negotiation with the other, and too easily becomes justification for eliminating any restrictions on what we can do to them, including killing and war. Combined with this, the temptation to ignore our own faults and considering ourselves essentially good quickly blinds us to suffering we may cause others, whether intentional or unintentional. Having introduced God into any conflict tends to solidify positions as sacred and making negoiation more difficult. Once the other is considered evil, we have evoked the image of God and Satan contending for the world.

In this instance both parties see themselves on God's side and therefore capable of doing no wrong to those on Satan's side. 'Killing' and 'torture' became a moral duty. One side kept escalating feelings about 'bin Laden' to 'Hussein', to 'al-Qaeda' to 'Islam'; while the other side escalated feelings about 'Bush' to all 'Americans', to 'America', and to 'Western Culture'. The 'rule of law' soon became 'Sharia law' to one, and 'law of self interest' to the other. One side 'seeking a Palestinian state' soon became 'seeking the elimination of the Israeli state', even as the other side 'aiding the Jews who suffered the holocaust' soon became 'ignoring the Palestinians' suffering'. One side called people 'Afghan freedom fighters' when they fought against Russia (Osama bin Laden was recruited during the Soviet-Afghan war by the CIA to fight the Soviet invaders), yet called the same people "terrorists" when they fought against America. The other side called pilots "God's agents" when they flew planes full of innocent people into buildings full of innocent workers at the WTC, but called pilots "agents of the Great Satan" when they dropped smart bombs on targeted buildings in Kabul. On our part, it became easy to have a double standard toward our friends and those we call enemies; we attacked Iraq when it invaded Kuwait, and kept a blind eye when Israel bulldozed Palestinian homes on the West Bank and ignored the UN resolutions requiring withdrawal from occupied territories. We condemned Islamic *fatwa* (religious edicts) but wanted bin Laden "dead or alive" without any judicial review, denying the very principles and values that we are supposed to represent. When our enemy was willing to kill or die for what they believed, we called them "Terrorists". But when our soldiers were willing to kill or die for what they believed, we called them "Patriots".

Fortunately, I had learned to expect that the incumbent administration's appeal to militant actions and retribution would be accompanied by much of the popular media's attention to short-term emotional and militant solutions to complicated problems. Having already publicly stated my thoughts about how we should respond, I was now determined to dig deeper for insights on how to respond to the events of 9/11.

I listened to the Dalai Lama suggest that we must choose to respond, not from fear, but from love, and not to pinpoint blame for terror, but to pinpoint the cause of it as the only way to escape the cycle of retribution. He said that ignoring the basic spiritual wisdom that the human race is all one, was to ignore the central teaching in most spiritual traditions: "What you wish to experience, provide for another". If you want peace, provide peace for another. If you wish safety for yourself, cause another to know they are safe. I also recalled Gandhi's words: "I object to violence because when it appears to do good, the good is only temporary. The evil it does is permanent." And King's words: "Returning violence for violence multiplies violence, adding deeper darkness to a night already devoid of stars. Darkness cannot drive out darkness, only light can do that. Hate cannot drive out hate; only love can do that." The BPF (Baptist Peace Fellowship) counseled the world leaders to seek justice through nonviolent means, and then committed themselves to the long-term response of "acting creatively for the ministry of reconciliation and building a culture of peace in our families, churches, communities, nations, and world." The FOR (Fellowship of Reconciliation) said that vengeance and retaliation simply increase the spiral of violence and perpetuate and deepen the culture of violence. It said: "It is a time to draw upon the deep resources of faith and to examine our lives in the light of the oneness of the human family and for the divine spirit that animates us all."

The Canadian Council of Churches reminded us that an international dimension to any trial is essential for bringing to justice those accused of the criminal acts of September 11, and that in bringing those accused of terrorism to justice: "In international relations the United Nations and its Security Council are the essential custodians of international due process, and that an exclusively American trial is unlikely to have the confidence of many states". It continued that: "Canada, with its clear commitment to multilateralism, can help the United States understand the need for it to re-engage with the world in support of collective security measures such as the International Criminal Court, the Kyoto environmental protocol, the Comprehensive (nuclear) Test-Ban Treaty and other similar measures"—all of which the United States had been failing to do. It stated further that: "A serious campaign against terrorism needs to address the social, economic and political conditions that tend to nurture the emergence of terrorism." And while it recognized the challenge to bring to justice those accused to trial, it declared that "the early characterization of the response to the terrorist attacks on the United States as 'war' misrepresents the nature of that challenge." It concluded that the United States response:

"does not require, and must not include, broad military attacks...Resort to military force well beyond police or police-support actions are well beyond the limits of international and humanitarian law. Canada cannot be a party to such actions."

It was heartening when a wide spectrum of over 100 American religious leaders signed 'A Religious Response to Terrorism', saying:

"We can deny Terrorists their victory by refusing to submit to a world created in their image. We assert the vision of community, tolerance, compassion, justice, and the sacredness of human life, which lies at the heart of all our religious traditions. Our American illusion of invulnerability has been shattered. This attack on our life as a nation will become a test of our national character. Let us rededicate ourselves to global peace, human dignity, and the eradication of injustice that breeds rage and vengeance."

In the year following 9/11/01 and prior to the Iraq war, I tried to understand 'Terrorism' and our response to it that we called the 'War on Terrorism', from the standpoint of my understanding of Active Nonviolence. I came to the conclusion that if the definition of a terrorist is anyone who murders an innocent civilian to send a political message, then the United States should also be considered a terrorist nation, when we consider our use of A-Bombs, fire-bombs or smart-bombs on civilian populations. 'Terrorism' to one group is 'self-defense' to another. Using the word 'terrorist' is laden with so much emotion that it is probably best not to use it, instead placing emphasis on the criminal acts rather than the character of those who do them. There are Muslims who do criminal (terrorist) acts, just as there are Christians or Jews and people of no religion who do criminal (terrorist) acts. However using 'Islamic terrorist', definitely should not be used, even as 'Christian terrorist' or 'Jewish terrorist' should not be used, associating the entire religion with the acts of a few. The focus must be kept on 'criminal acts', not on 'persons'.

My commitment to 'Active Nonviolence' begins with the belief that we are all children of God. That includes both President Bush and Mr. Bin Laden. Active Nonviolence rejects labeling others as "enemies" and instead sees them as opponents who are also "children of God", worthy of respect and potential friends. When anyone is backed into a corner with harsh denunciations, they will try to save face by defending themselves and refuse to listen or consider opposing arguments. This becomes especially dangerous when God is enlisted in supporting their side against others. Further, declaring that if you are not for us, you are against us labels them as evil, against God, justice, truth, and righteousness. Such rhetoric soon justifies almost any action one takes, including the use of violence to overcome that evil. Both President Bush and Mr. Bin Laden use such logic, resulting in their respective actions. However, violence is never the answer, whether criminal acts of terrorism or wars against terrorism. Simply put, no one wins from violence and no one wins from war. There is no such thing as 'redemptive violence', but only a continuing 'spiral of violence'. Rather than dropping bombs in Afghanistan, Active Nonviolence would drop food and medicines on the poor, bringing smiles rather than hatred. Mr. Bin Laden is a 'child of God' regardless of how we regard his actions. However, all criminal acts, and those who do them, should be prosecuted through legal court systems or international tribunals, not by war and killing. He and his 'criminal acts' must be judged before the proper courts of law. We know how the Bush Administration proceeded after 9/11: Go to war against the Terrorists in Afghanistan. The plan was to end terrorism by killing its leaders and all who enabled their efforts. The solution was again the response of 'redemptive violence', the age-old practice of trying to end violence through the use of violence.

The Bush Administration ignored the wisdom of the 1960s Kerner Report. It said that race riots were simply the predictable result of racial injustice, of a nation increasingly being divided into rich-whites and poor-blacks. The violence of those riots were likened to the destructive lava flowing from the top of the erupting volcano of racial and social inequality, and that the only lasting solution was to address the injustice of racial inequalities.

The Administration also ignored the wisdom of Dom Helder Camara's 'Spiral of Violence' that Camara saw happening in the third world countries of Latin America. The violence of revolt and revolution, he said, is simply the result of a prior more basic violence, the violence of injustice existing in the status quo controlled by those who have power. Those who benefit from the existing stability and order of their society tend to focus attention on the violence of revolt and try to suppress it, usually with the violence of militant force. However the only lasting solution to the violence of revolt is to address the prior violence of injustice in the status quo, as our own U.S. Declaration of Independence declared: "Whenever any form of government becomes destructive of those ends, it is the right of the people to alter or abolish it...it is their right, it their duty, to throw off such government and to provide new guards for their future security." Camara would have agreed that we seek to bring those responsible for 9/11 to justice, but would have advised our Government not to focus on defending the injustices of our international public policies around the world, and to focus on the causes of the anger of those who feel oppressed and denied power and justice by a world dominated by U.S. power.

Cesar Chavez would have said: "We are only just beginning to understand the power of love and nonviolence because we are just beginning to understand the weakness of force and oppression." Pope Paul VI would have said: "If you want peace, work for justice." Martin Luther King, Jr. would have said: "One day we must come to see that peace is not merely a distant goal that we seek, but that it is a means by which we arrive at the goal. We must pursue peaceful ends through peaceful means." Gandhi would have said: "You must be the change you want to see in the world." And Jesus would have said: "Love your enemies."

So how should we proceed after 9/11? Whatever we do, stopping terrorist acts must be done simultaneously as we uphold our moral values and it must not be for retribution. Retribution is what terrorists do. We must understand 9/11 as an act of retribution against us for what they see as our evil doings. Our response must not be one of retribution. We won't defeat terrorism with more of the violence of bombs and killings. We must realize that our massive military spending and weapons are mostly useless. Every time we kill a civilian we breed anti-American feelings, sowing the seeds of future terrorists and increasing the resentments that produce the demand for retribution.

We must proceed, not by how we use army tanks to fight wars, but more of how we fight mosquitoes. You don't win the battle against mosquitoes by killing them one at a time, or hundreds at a time. You can only defeat mosquitoes by removing their breeding grounds or swamps. Malaria, whether in the swamps and water of Panama or Africa or our own backyards and community, can only be controlled by eliminating the source of mosquito origination that leads to their proliferation. That source is stagnant water. Not water which is essential for life, but a stagnant water. Likewise, the source of the mosquitoes of terrorism is poverty in a world of affluence, hunger in a world capable of food abundance, injustice in a world demanding justice.

Perhaps John Lederach, Professor of Conflict Studies, who uses the metaphor of the image of a virus, has suggested an even better metaphor for defeating terrorism. A virus has the ability to enter a system unperceived and to flow within it to harm it from within, whether in a human body or in a computer. You don't fight this kind of system by shooting at it, but by strengthening the system's capacity to prevent the virus and increase the system's immunity. The virus that results in terrorism is the anger and frustration of people who have experienced over time sustained injustice from historical events that have excluded them from a hopeful future. It is this exclusion that provides the soil and seedbed for leaders like Osama bin Laden to cultivate and exploit to recruit future terrorists.

Our responding to terrorists with military might is a totally wrong approach to the problem. It only reinforces the anger of those who feel excluded, providing fresh soil for increased terrorist recruitment, and seems to prove their leaders contention that we are out to destroy them. I remember John Steinbeck's 'The Grapes of Wrath' describing one of the 'Okies' saying:

> "Somepin went an' happened to me when they tol' me I had to get off the place. First I was gonna go in an' kill a

whole flock a people...go in town and kill folks. 'Cause what'd they take when they tractored the folks off the lan'? What'd they get so their 'margin a profit' was safe? God knows the lan' ain't no good. Nobody been able to make a crop for years. But them sons-a-bitches at their desks, they jus' chopped folks in two for their margin a profit."

What was true in the 1930s in California is just as true in Afghanistan and other countries with massive poverty. We must understand how people come to this anger, hatred and frustration if we wish to overcome terrorism. Our response of force and military power only reinforces their anger, fulfills their expectations of us trying to destroy them, and increases future cycles of revenge and violence. Our emphasis in combating terrorism must be in removing the causes of anger that attracts and sustains their efforts. The traditional weapons of war are useless. Even focusing our efforts on the terrorists and their leaders is counterproductive. Our focus must be on the people of Afghanistan and surrounding countries, developing constructive relationships and offering to help meet their basic needs, so as to eliminate the conditions that breed terrorists.

Unfortunately, following 9/11, we as a nation acquiesced in the disastrous and downright wrong policies of the Bush administration and the failure of our Congress to resist them. The traditional revenge pattern soon began escalating the appeal to fear and called for extension of war to Iraq. Religious and secular peace oriented groups called for resistance to this insane escalation of war. Part of my efforts to support this included supporting Sacramento Peace Action, Veterans for Peace, and other secular groups, as well as supporting religious groups such as FOR, IPM, the Council of Churches and others, and specifically my own Lutheran community.

Versions of the following article were printed in several magazines, Letters to the Editors in newspapers, and sent to many pastors:

"WAR ON IRAQ—A KAIROS MOMENT

Today we in the United States face a crisis, the threatened war on Iraq. I believe it is a Kairos Moment! A Kairos Moment is a moment of truth, a moment of judgment, a moment of grace and opportunity, a time in which God issues a challenge to decisive action.

Our Bishop gave us guidance that "It is wrong for the U.S. to seek to overthrow the regime of Saddam Hussein with military action. Morally, I oppose it." The editor of The Lutheran courageously said, "Loyalty to Christ, I believe, requires us to say No, to this war." My observation, however, is that most pastors have been silent on this, possibly intimidated by popular support for war.

We Lutherans should have learned from the German Church struggles 60-70 years ago. Paul Lehmann said of that struggle "There must have been a moment, somewhere near the beginning, when we could have said no, but somehow we missed it."

In 1943 a small group of German church leaders had issued the Barman Synod's Declaration, saying that confession of Jesus Christ, as Lord required their theologically based resistance to Hitler and the Nazi regime. However, we know that the rising signs of fascism were not taken seriously, and most of the church capitulated, not willing to face the connection between theological confession and political resistance. Bonhoeffer scholar Eberhard Bethge said: "We resisted by confessing, but the difficult boundary to cross is when you begin to confess by resisting."

Numerous studies among Lutherans have been held regarding the historic Lutheran position of Just War and the threatened war on Iraq. Invariably the conclusion has been that a war on Iraq is unjustified. The criteria of just cause, proper authorization, intent, last resort and proportionality are not met in this situation. Further, many Lutherans, and the Lutheran Peace Fellowship as a group of thousands, believe that in the era of Weapons of Mass Destruction no war can be seriously considered as *just*, especially when *first strike* and *pre-emptive* military action is proposed. Responsible Christians call for the alternative of Active Nonviolence to this crisis. Fortunately, the leaders of most churches have spoken to this. We can be proud that our Church has taken a leading role in this. We pastors, in our congregations, must speak and act also.

- submitted by Rev. Dr. Jerry Pedersen, Jan. 21, 2003."

I was disheartened when on March 17, 2003, Congress voted to launch war against Iraq. It had been 18 months since 9/11/01 and our poorly directed fighting in Afghanistan had failed to accomplish anything worthwhile. The Bush Administrations had carefully attempted to script a link connecting Iraq to the 9/11 attack on the New York Trade Center and then used discredited evidence for their having Nuclear Weapons. However, a great deal of resistance against starting this war had taken place, not only by millions of people in the streets of America, but also by millions in the cities around the world. Likewise, leaders of many different religions, including unprecedented numbers of Christians, had strongly advocated against this war. Likewise, many in congress had spoken strongly against war, yet, when it came to a showdown, they voted for war. How did this happen?

Undoubtedly the fear generated by the terrorism of 9/11 was an important factor. However, even though this fear had been carefully aroused and capitalized on to gather support for the war, I believe fear was insufficient in itself to overcome opposition to it. I believe it was our habitual reliance on using *Redemptive Violence* for resolving such conflicts that enabled our going into this war. As a nation we had not yet learned that the darkness of terrorism cannot be overcome with violence. As Martin Luther King had often reminded us, using violence will not lead us out of darkness into light. Only love can do that. Using violence only leads to greater darkness.

However, neither fear nor reliance on our habitual use of *Redemptive Violence* is sufficient to explain our going into the Iraq war. The Iraq war was part of a plan that had been developing for over twenty years by a small group in our government determined to control our foreign policy. During the Reagan administration their efforts were to build up our military establishment, pushing us into invasions of Panama and Grenada and promoting counter-insurgency in Central America, arming Iraq to better fight Iran, and pushing for a final confrontation with Russia in the Cold War—in short, to promote American domination by the threat of pre-emptive war and threatening and controlling nuclear weapons. During the first Bush administration they demonstrated the United States being the lone superpower in the first Gulf War, emphasizing 'pre-emption' rather than 'curtailment' as our foreign policy, and using unilateral military power under the guise of multilateral and international cooperation. When they were unable to push the first Bush administration to follow through with the occupation of Iraq, and later failing to stop the Clinton administration's practice of multilateralism, this same group of people who were the "power behind the throne" formulated their "Project for a New American Century" and a "Global Pax Americana". It advocated an American rather than a United Nations dominated world, military might capable of fighting multiple wars and controlling domestic conflict and terrorism threats around the world, and removing Saddam Hussein from power in Iraq. Before the new century began, their plans for an "American Empire" were largely ignored at the time, and even they acknowledged that their plans were not likely to be accepted "absent some catastrophic and catalyzing event like a new Pearl Harbor". Shortly after the century began, that "new Pearl Harbor" happened on 9/11, instigating the Bush administration's War on Terrorism and war in Afghanistan. Within days "the powers" called for the elimination of Saddam Hussein, the real reason for his elimination being simply because their dream of an American Empire demanded it. And within a few months, President George Bush, in his State of the Union address in 2002, spoke of the War on Terrorism demanding the stoppage of the "Axis of Evil", Iraq, Iran and North Korea, which eventually became the Iraq War.

The full realization of all that had happened only became fully clear for me when I was able to obtain a copy of "The National

Security Strategy of the United States of America" that was published under the Presidential Seal in September 2002. As I began reading it, I was at first encouraged when the overview began with: "Our nation's cause has always been larger than our Nation's defense. We fight, as we always fight, for a just peace, we will extend the peace by encouraging free and open societies on every continent." I soon became apprehensive however when it quoted from President Bush's September 14, 2001 speech: "Just three days removed from these events, Americans do not yet have the distance of history. But our responsibility to history is already clear: to answer these attacks and rid the world of evil. This nation is peaceful. The conflict was begun on the timing and terms of others. It will end in a way, and at an hour, of our choosing."

"To rid the world of evil!" Really, is ridding the world of evil our task as a nation? Dare we assume that we are a peaceful nation, that we are 'the good' as over against 'the evil'? As I read on, I became convinced that this was a most 'un-American, undemocratic, immoral strategy' when it read "we will not hesitate to act alone", "acting preemptively against terrorists", "prevent adversaries military build-up equaling the power of the U.S.", or "we do not accept investigations, inquiry, or prosecution by the International Criminal Court (ICC)" and much other unacceptable strategy. The strategy articulated there was entirely a militaristic strategy, the strategy of *Redemptive Violence*, and a strategy that relied on the *Love of Power*, whereas I was convinced that the only successful strategy was trusting in the *Power of Love*. Lacking in our national security strategy was any positive steps toward a more peaceful world such as had been envisioned in the plans of the United Nations for the International Decade for a Culture of Peace and Nonviolence or its Millennium Development Goals for the elimination of poverty. Instead, we were ignoring those plans, and in fact acting in ways that would insure their failure, by doing exactly the wrong thing, nurturing the seedbeds of recruitment for further terrorists. Osama bin Laden and the Al Queda couldn't have been more pleased.

As the Iraq War continued on for two, three, four, and now over five years, I was astonished how easily we all had become accommodated to it. On many occasions I had spoken sharply to this fact, even suggesting that we were like the citizens of Germany during the 1930s and early1940s who could ignore the presence of Hitler's concentration camps, with the smoke rising from their incinerators killing bodies of the Holocaust victims, and the preparations for and then conducting their horrible war. When saying this to secular groups, I had my patriotism questioned. When saying to church groups, and ministerial groups, I usually encountered silence, even when I knew that the majority of them opposed the war, as though I was the extremist, unrealistic and unnecessary troublemaker. Even among the members of a Forum group, people who were well informed and committed to social activism and moral values, I typically encountered resignation to the war and their feelings of helplessness to do anything about it. My proposals to study and promote Active Nonviolence usually fell on deaf ears and apathy. I kept remembering Martin Luther King's statement: "He who passively accepts evil is as much involved in it as he who helps to perpetrate it. He who accepts evil without protesting against it is really cooperating with it." Likewise the words of my martyred hero Bishop Oscar Romero of El Salvador: "A church that does not provoke any crisis, preach a gospel that does not unsettle, proclaim a word of God that does not get under anyone's skin or a word of God that does not touch the real sin of the society in which it is being proclaimed: what kind of gospel is that?"

Increasingly, I decided my efforts must be less toward the negative protest against war, and more toward the positive effort to promote a commitment to active nonviolence. As long as people believed that violence could be redemptive, the flow of adrenaline generated by the emotional appeal of war would continue to be utilized by militarists to mobilize the mass of people to support their questionable goal of peace by the use of violence. I began this effort by researching again a study and report made at Stanford University's School of Medicine by a Committee on Violence. They undertook their task, not as moralists, but as a group of behavioral scientists. Their conclusion was:

"Violence is not an inherited trait. It can be understood and controlled. Man can now, for the first time in history, take charge of his own evolution; his destiny need no longer be imposed from without. Once we perform the revolutionary but simple act of deciding that we can truly change, the era of violence can close."

Their point of view was that our behavior could be best explained as a struggle to adapt to our surroundings. They understood aggression as a positive assertive behavior necessary for survival. In the early stages of human evolution, as a nomadic hunter in an environment of hostile tribes and animals, and even later in an agricultural and sedentary struggle amid food scarce nature, this aggression was often violent. However, under these circumstances the violence was adaptive behavior helping to survive. As we moved from a pre-agricultural age through the agricultural age to the industrial age and now to our technological age, we still continue to use violent aggression that was appropriate for the earlier pre-agricultural age, but that is no longer appropriate in trying to meet conditions in our technological age. Technology has increasingly helped us change our environment, yet we have not been able to change the conditions necessary for our survival fast enough to adapt to the environmental changes we have made. Our present task is to learn how to manage our behavior in this changing environment: that is, to take control of our own evolution.

It is encouraging to know that, although they believe this is a difficult task, it is not impossible. During times of extreme stressful situations people are easily tempted to resort to aggressive violent behavior, whether beating their children or going to war, in trying to manage their lives. However, it is such times, unless we are simply overwhelmed by the stress, that often provide peak learning opportunities to find more adaptive solutions to these extreme situations. We know that crisis can have constructive as well as destructive possibilities. Instead of retreating into primitive forms of behavior that simply blames others and lashes out in violence, it is possible to channel aggressive energy into more constructive forms of adaptive behavior. In other words, our problem is one of violence, not aggression. Our task is to find ways to utilize the energy of aggression, and not let it be turned towards primitive violence.

The Stanford report suggested a number of ways to make the U.S. a more adaptive society. They found that among all vertebrates, including humans, that overcrowding produces uncontrolled aggression. They found that violence shown in mass media too often wrongly teaches children (and adults) that violence is appropriate adaptive behavior, and this therefore, needs to be diminished and stripped of its glamour. Recognizing that guns once helped settle this country and was adaptive behavior in a frontier society, they said possession of guns illustrate the changing nature of adaptive behavior in our complex urban society, and some form of gun control is now essential. However, what especially caught my attention was their concept of 'collective sanctioned violence'. They make the case that the sanctioning war and capital punishment breeds deadly confusion by condemning some forms of killing while valuing other forms. Especially, our nation's high valuation of military glory and our acceptance of sanctioned violence as an effective means of resolving conflict—guarantees that violent behavior will continue. The psychology of sanctioned violence depends on our attributing evil motives to others, thereby justifying the violence we perpetrate on them: because they are violent (evil), and we are good, it is necessary and acceptable for us to be violent (evil) toward them. Sanctioning or justifying the use of violence for societal or national problems in order to promote good order or achieve justice, too easily also becomes permission for individuals to use violence to solve their individual problems.

The Stanford report concludes that use of sanctioned violence must become totally unacceptable for our national and societal problems, especially a reliance on war and capital punishment. Likewise, it finds that sanctioning parental use of violence to punish children must end, constructive channels must be developed and utilized for expressing healthy aggression in 'conflict resolution' and peaceful protests, more use made of using an 'ombudsman' to deal with complaints, changing the teaching of history from being the record of a steady procession of wars to being the evolving developments of a healthy society, and shifting the emphasis regarding crime to prevention and rehabilitation rather than punishment.

In this time of discouragement for me as our nation wallowed in a disastrous war of choice and not a war of necessity, the Stanford report became a component of classes and training I participated in and led in Active Nonviolence. In the midst of the fear deliberately foisted on the public by an administration anxious to extend the American Empire around the globe, I needed the support that a reputable scientific study like the Stanford report provided concerning violence—that it is not an inherited trait, that it can be controlled, and that for the first time in history the era of violence could come to a close, even though this will take time and not come easily.

Fortunately, we also had access to the brilliant work of Dr. R.M. Kidder. Based on countless interviews, he has come to a very positive view of human nature, and like the Stanford study, believes change and positive growth has happened and can continue happening. Basic in his thinking is that people all over the country, whether rich or poor, Democrats or Republicans, rural or urban, whether religious or not, and irrespective of people's religion, all have the same core values: honesty, responsibility, fairness, respect, and compassion. Likewise, in making ethical decisions, he finds it is not helpful thinking in terms of good and bad, or right verses wrong. Rather, a strong moral argument can usually be made on both sides of really tough decisions, and to force people to think that only one side is right often misses the demands of both justice and peace. As I earlier described, in my experience in Africa of wise old tribal leaders brought to the University for short term upgrading as magistrates in Western Judicial Practices, I often found them laughing at our practices in law. They rejected the goal of punishment, of finding who was right and who was wrong. Their goal in tribal matters was to restore right relations and community and reconciliation. Rather than our Western practice of one party feeling angry that the decision had gone against them while the other party celebrated victory, tribal society had both parties celebrating together with *pombe* and dancing in renewed community. In the same way, Kidder advocates a 'right versus right' model, instead of a 'right versus wrong' model, as a more scientific and effective model for the process of making moral decisions.

Kidder's concept of a 'moral perimeter' I found especially helpful. He uses it to explain why, despite people having the same shared values, there is so much fighting and conflict and unethical behavior in our society. He says that each of us operate our lives as though a circle surrounds us, within which people have our profound moral concern. Outside that circle, for whatever reason, people don't receive our moral concern. That circle is our 'moral perimeter'. Inside the perimeter, even a disreputable person, such as a criminal brother, has our concern, whereas outside the perimeter, no one has our moral concern, no matter who they are. He uses the Mafia as an example: within the brotherhood there is a sense of responsibility and compassion for one another, but outside the brotherhood those values don't matter.

Our task then as individual and as a society is to expand the moral perimeter. The history of civilization is the history of expanding perimeters. Fortunately, the history of our nation has also been one of constantly expanding the moral perimeter, although it has only come about through great struggle. The movements abolishing slavery, racial discrimination, women's suffrage, labor rights, homosexuality, and conscientious objection all are efforts to expand culturally the moral perimeters of our people, and all still have a long way to go. I have tried to present Active Nonviolence as the practice of extending one's moral perimeter to all people as though there were none outside to it. Good leadership ought to have this characteristic. The life of Jesus can be seen as a good example of this, as were the lives of Gandhi and Martin Luther King and Cesar Chavez and Dorothy Day and other advocates of nonviolence. And the United Nations and the Interfaith Religious Initiative are examples of the efforts of nations and religions seeking to expand their moral perimeters to be more inclusive.

I wonder whether the Crisis in this first decade of the century will lead to constructive or destructive change. What started with such high hopes for creating a culture of peace and nonviolence and overcoming world hunger, got side tracked by an act of terrorism. Perhaps the hope was only an illusion, the reality being that a powerful small group of neo-cons were bent on creating an American Empire to dominate the world, not for peace and justice, but for their love of power instead of for the power of love. Perhaps the hope was only an illusion, the reality being that Eisenhower's warning of an industrial/military/financial/corporation complex had come to pass, undermining democracy, freedom, and the constitution. Perhaps the hope was only an illusion, the reality being that evil forces are so powerful that the power of darkness is snuffing out the forces of light.

Or perhaps this Crisis is truly a Kairos Moment, a time of opportunity for creating new ways of living, a time when we are called by God to take charge of our own evolution and begin living as truly social beings, understanding that this is a moral universe, and we have the capacity to live more humanly within it. It is often in times of crisis that the peak moments of creative energy are liberated to work toward ending an era of violence so that a more true community might become a reality. That is my hope, and for that I am committed.

"You must be the change you want to see in the world."

—Gandhi

Chapter 10

SEPTEMBER 2, 2008: Hope Renewed

ON SEPTEMBER 2, 2008, it had been 63 years since that September 2nd in 1945 when I had been part of the Honor Guard at the Peace Surrender of the Japanese aboard the USS Missouri in Tokyo Bay at the end of World War II. I had witnessed General Douglas MacArthur sign the Surrender Document from the Japanese, and heard him say: "We must go forward to preserve in peace what we won in war" which was instrumental in my setting out on a Journey of Peacemaking.

Now I needed time and a place to reflect on my journey, and decided to return to Glacier Point above Yosemite Valley. It had been over 70 years since the first time I had stepped out at Glacier Point to watch the sun rise over the valley. As I again looked out on this fantastic view, two thoughts crossed my mind: first, the words of Pere Teilhard de Chardin from his 'Hymn of the Universe', and second, the question I had asked earlier in the summer when I had again visited Glacier Point: when had it all changed?

Pere Teilhard, the man of science, was also a man of prayer, who used the poetical language of the mystic when, looking with the eye of the scientist, he saw the presence of the Creator everywhere and in everything throughout the material world. Ever since I first read the following words in 'Hymn of the Universe' Teilhard had written while on a scientific expedition out in the Ordos desert in the deepest part of China, I too was enabled to better reverence the material world while being aware of the spiritual within it:

"Since once again, Lord, I have neither bread, nor wine, nor altar, I will raise myself beyond these symbols, up to the pure majesty of the real itself; I, your priest, will make the whole earth my altar and on it will offer you all the labours and sufferings of the world...Through your own incarnation, my God, all matter is henceforth incarnate...But the offering you really want, the offering you mysteriously need every day to appease your hunger, to slake your thirst is nothing less than the growth of the world borne ever onwards in the stream of universal becoming."

Pere Teilhard saw matter as the matrix of spirit, creation as an evolutionary process, an inexhaustible potentiality for existence and transformation. From a totally difference perspective, Sir Julian Huxley had called this "progressive psychosocial evolution", the process of man's potentialities more and more realized, so that all the forces of the animal world are progressively spiritualized in human development. Teilhard's conviction led him to see:

"That man holds in his hands the fortunes of the universe, and immediately you cause him to turn his face towards the grandeur of a new sunrise. Let him once discover that his fate is bound up with the fate of nature itself, and immediately, joyously, he will begin again his forward march."

It was the renewal of this "grandeur of a new sunrise" that I needed. Increasingly I had been discovering that it was not only the fate of humanity that was bound up with our abandoning violence as a means of coping with conflict, but also the "fate of nature itself", if we were to march forward "in the stream of universal becoming"

Following WWII, I had set off on my peacemaking journey "to preserve in peace what we had won in war". Although after the turn of the century, the discouragement of all that had happened with war and its effects required a renewal of my hopes for moving "onwards in the stream of universal becoming", of "joyously beginning again the forward march", to "turn my face towards the grandeur of a new sunrise." The sunrise I observed over Yosemite Valley matched the renewal of hope I was now experiencing.

This renewal of hope was the answer to my question—when had it all changed? I guess I'm a slow learner, slow to realize that the world hadn't changed; only my perception of a soft, cozy, secure world out there had changed. That perception was an illusion.

The seeds for peacemaking were planted early in my life through loving and caring family relationships, and cultivated in my teens at Confirmation to follow the Way of Jesus, and then as an Eagle Scout taking the oath to Honor God and Country. Further, I had understood that my country America was the bearer of those same values, a model that we wanted to share with world. When the bombing of Pearl Harbor happened on December 7, 1941 as a threat to all this, I joined the Marine Corps as soon as possible to fight the war in the Pacific thinking this was the path to peace, realizing along the way that my "safe, cozy, secure world" wasn't as secure as I had imagined. Then, aboard the Battleship Missouri on September 2nd, 1945, as an Honor Guard at the Peace Surrender Signing by the Japanese, I heard General Douglas MacArthur say: "There can be no turning back...We must go forward to preserve in peace what we have won in war." And I read the words again that Admiral William F. Halsey had addressed to us: "We must establish a peace, a firm, a just, and an enduring peace." That day I made the decision to be a peacemaker. Later I would receive a good education, enter a very good marriage, have children, and be considered successful.

However, along the way I began to realize that I had been naïve and unrealistic about my "safe, cozy, secure world." It took awhile to realize the truth of what my Dad had one time said, "the nice, soft, purring cat, also scratches". Although I was determined to keep my commitment of seeking to be a peacemaker, I had to learn along the way an important lesson: There is no way to peace—peace is the way.

Learning how to be a peacemaker has been an ongoing struggle, beginning with my choice of vocation. I believed my 'calling' was to be a 'peacemaker', and specifically as an 'anti-war' oriented maker of peace. Among the options I considered for pursuing that objective were teacher, politician, minister, counselor, social worker, labor organizer, and youth worker among other possibilities, before finally deciding on the ministry. Coming from a protestant and Lutheran family, it was natural to think of ministry as becoming a pastor, the term we used rather than reverend, priest or minister. However, in our family being a 'pastor' also included being called 'preach', a term that didn't appeal to me at all. Likewise, doing 'priestly' functions dispensing sacraments at the altar or at the baptismal font were not my highest priority. And administrative duties were not my thing, although I increasingly discovered that such duties demanded my attention and time, as I observed happening to many of my colleagues who seemed to gravitate toward managerial roles, a role that I rejected as much as possible. Being "Pastor Jerry" had a good feel to it, and for a time I truly enjoyed the warm strokes I felt when called that.

However I soon began to understand that being 'pastor' to people had strings attached, or at least I felt it did. It seemed people felt that my task was to primarily make people 'comfortable', and although I very much wanted to "bring comfort to the afflicted" in cases of illness, hunger, poverty, unemployment and suffering, I found many people rather comfortable in the stagnation of living lives accommodated to injustice and found myself more and more "afflicting the comfortable," or at least trying to help them discover transforming experiences. I didn't want to "shepherd the sheep", or "tend the flock", or deal with people as 'children', and I endeavored to deal with people as responsible adults who wanted to be part of a 'creative community' and especially wanted to be part of a community of fellow peacemakers.

One of the lessons that I had to learn was the same lesson most people and nations have to learn. Great confusion comes from false understandings of Peace. For instance, peace is not simply the absence of war. When war ends, that doesn't necessarily mean peace is achieved. At the end of WWII, to "preserve the Peace" for too many people simply meant, "keeping the absence of war". Beginning the United Nations, and instituting the Marshall Plan, were genuine efforts to promote peace, continuing the militarism begun during the war years, later identified by President Eisenhower as the

Military/Industrial Complex, and the start of the Cold War that was to continue for 45 years, and an Arms Race that still continues, and establishing monetary practices that insured a growing gap between the Undeveloped Countries and the West, were all denials "of preserving the peace".

I also soon realized that my religious understanding of peace needed to be enlarged. I was to learn that at the heart of all major religions, and particularly for the religions of the Book—Jews, Christians and Muslims—the same word Shalom, Peace or Salaam, refers to a wholeness concept covering private and public, individual and social, religious and secular—that is, all relationships. It is not the 'absence' of something, but the 'presence' of something: good health, long life, a full stomach, a roof over your head, family, security, employment, and a life of joy and hope and justice. I particularly had to learn that the 'inner' personal peace I had experienced through my faith, while highly cherished as a free gift given to me, had to be seriously enlarged to include also the challenge to work for peace in the 'outer' social world.

Likewise, my religious understanding of peace needed to include how I viewed other religions. While I needed to grow in appreciation and understanding of the particularity of my own faith, I needed to better understand and recognize the validity of other expressions of religious faith, and learn from them. As theologian Hans Kung said: "There will be no peace among the nations without peace among the religions." My own commitment to peace and my own faith have been deepened and richly blessed by exposure to others: the Jewish emphasis on justice and "tikkun olam" (repairing the world), Buddhism's emphasis on compassion and centeredness, Islam's concern for the poor, Native American reverence for Mother Earth and nature, Humanist's concern for freedom and community, the Catholic's ethical emphasis on the Common Cause and the Quaker's emphasis on nonviolence, and many others.

I have had to learn that peace is like life itself, not static but alive and dynamic, a process, and a way of life. The image of someone at a funeral saying "he looks so peaceful" as they look at the body lying in the casket simply doesn't describe peace. A better image might be a painting of a wild turbulent waterfall with a small branch jutting out from it with a little bird sitting on the branch, chirping exuberantly and joyfully celebrating life—peace is being able to celebrate life even in the midst of all the inevitable turmoils, conflicts and setbacks of life. It was this insight that led me to declare my life's motto as "Dare to Dance in the Midst of Life!—and then adding after discovering the dissidence that life offered—"no matter how deep the bad gets."

This change for me came about, not in one cataclysmic moment, but in a multitude of small incremental steps. Peace for an individual must necessarily continually renew itself, ever as a healthy human body is continually renewing itself or it soon becomes unhealthy. And what is true for persons is likewise true for all communities or society. Likewise, my 'inner peace' continues to be a valuable resource for my life, yet has constantly had to be reexamined and attuned to life's realities, even as the world's peace will not be some final or utopian achievement, but an unfolding expression of the "stream of universal becoming" and the "grandeur of a new sunrise."

What I included in my commitment to peace also had to go through a growing process. At first, for me, peace consisted of the 'inner' peace of my faith and the 'outer' peace regarding war. However, my peacemaking soon confronted the many other dimensions of peace. The Pope had said, "If you want peace, work for justice," and it didn't take long for racial issues to claim my attention, whether for Civil Rights in America, in educational developments in Africa, or race and education concerns at S.F. State University. During this time, I had little awareness of Women's Issues, and the injustices of feminist's concerns finally exploded on me during the strike at SFSU. In the midst of all the conflict, student arrests, community anger, administration's accusations, and my own arrest and trial, I was daily confronted with 'my insensitivity' to the concerns of women, whether it was my reference to them as 'gals', consenting to their lower pay scales, or for not objecting to the lack of more women leaders among the strikers. When I appealed for a little more understanding because of all the pressures I was under, I got little sympathy, and was reminded that women had to live with that reality all the time. Hopefully I made some personal progress then in my awareness of women's issues, and have since grown fully aware and committed to women's rights, yet I try to always remember the difficulty I had overcoming my unrecognized prejudice of "male privilege" and realize that I still am not totally free of it.

One of the things that doesn't seem to change is the existence of poor people in the world. In America, at least, there was real hope for change in the 1960s when our nation seemed to be ready to embrace President Johnson's 'War on Poverty'. This included rejecting the old Victorian view that poverty was primarily the personal moral failure of the poor themselves, and was rather the failure of the repressive systemic structures of our society as a whole. However it wasn't long before the high financial costs of our nation's militarization as well as the high cost in human lives and the backlash from the Vietnam War resulted in the conservative ideology of the 1980s and the bogus "Welfare Reforms" of the 1990s which rejected the morality which credited injustice and oppression as the cause of poverty, and instead returned to the Victorian era morality which credited poverty as being caused by the failure of personal behavior.

Then, at the turn of the century, when the United Nations adopted the 'Millennium Development Goals' for the new Century, which aimed at seriously reducing world poverty, I again had high hopes for serious change, both in America and the world. However, following 9/11, it became abundantly clear that "the powers" dictating American policies did not have the elimination of poverty as its goal, but rather the enhancement of the wealth of the powerful. Early in the new century, despite the well-known fact that each day 16,000 children die from hunger-related causes, America rejected the proposal of Bread for the World—a proposal that we allot a mere 3% of the money we spend each year on our military budget, or as little as 10% of the money in tax cuts we gave to the wealthiest 1% of Americans in 2002, to be spent on basic health and nutrition needs of the world's poor people to largely end that desperate situation.

Serious peacemaking necessitates that we deal with this issue of poverty and the poor as a top priority and moral issue, whether viewed from a Constitutional point of view of "justice for all" or from a Biblical point of view of the sacredness of individual life. And that begins with changing the oppressive structures and entrenched interests that perpetuate poverty in America, as well as throughout the world. The personal behavioral changes called for to eliminate poverty should not start with the poor and powerless in our society, but rather with the wealthy and powerful. It was not the poor that Jesus drove out of the temple, it was the moneychangers. God's concern and love is for all, yet in the relationships of rich and poor God stands on the side of the poor. An economy that favors the moneychangers, the wealthy and the financial interests of America must be changed, and that means structural changes. And, if personal behavioral changes need to be made, they must be demanded first of all from those who possess the power.

My journey of peacemaking has led me to become less concerned about believing 'who' Jesus was, and more about believing in his way of living and its importance for us. I have come to see Jesus as one who created a 'New Way of Living' in relation to power, money, race, war, violence. His "New Way of Living" rejected the political realism of the Sadducees and the revolutionary violence of the Zealots, as well as the escapism of the Esseens and the piety of the Pharisees. His "New Way of Living" and his advocating it for others has similarities to "Ways" found among all world religions. I believe this "Way" is the basis of hope for the poor and for overcoming poverty.

The hope for poor people today won't come from 'development' based on values and models devised by the rich or powerful to preserve and enhance their own privileges. Hopes for the poor will only come from a New Way of Living, a 'liberation' where the poor use their own energies to work for their own welfare. Recognizing that those in power do not willingly give up privileges that deny hope for the poor unless forced to do so, the poor themselves must not see themselves as victims without power, and assert their resistance to the prevailing power structures that is within their power. What Jesus called "the Kingdom of God" was more than a new system or political order, even though its radical meaning brings revolution to any social order, while at the same time retaining prophetic judgment and caution toward any specific new revolutionary order. It was a "New Way of Living" with prophetic implications for rich and poor alike, and profound political implications leading to militant opposition and crucifixion. Martin Luther King called this "New Way of Living" the "Community of the Beloved", and said it was the basis of a new social order being born. While leading people in nonviolent actions in this new way of living, he declared: "We stand between two worlds, the dying Old and the emerging New," and in doing this he made himself a candidate for militant opposition and assassination by those determined to retain the advantages they enjoyed in the Old ways.

From the perspective of this 'New Way of Living' what America suffered on 9/11 was what others throughout the world, especially the poor of the earth, had already experienced earlier in history at the hands of Western powers and more recently at the hands of America. Killing people with bombs is a "hot" form of violence, while exploiting people during the earlier colonial era or during our later neo-colonial era is a "soft" form of violence, but violence nonetheless. Winning a war against terrorism will only happen when we recognize our part in it, and begin waging war on the roots of terrorism: poverty, exploitation, hunger, disease and greed. What we have been doing is the 'Old Way of Living'. Terrorism does not happen in a vacuum. It happens when political and social and economic conditions become so unjust and institutionalized that anger, discontent and opposition are desperately expressed against them. Military force, retribution, suppression, all forms of violence against the desperation caused by enforcement of the Old Way, only drives those who suffer to greater anger and responsive violence, feeling it is the only thing they can do to resist the exploitation. Archbishop Helder Camara described this as the 'Cycle of Violence', and the 'Kerner Report' described it as the cause of violence, and our 'Declaration of Independence' described it as cause for peoples to rebel. The Old Way of Living doesn't work in our modern world. The time is ripe for a New Way of Living.

I had always taken pride in my commitment to basing my thoughts and actions on truth and being ready to abandon any that were untruthful. Like the time that I was advocating a more 'socialistic' salary scale for all pastors, rather than being based on what individual congregations were able to pay, since some were able to pay much more than other congregations, causing some pastors to suffer inadequate pay. At the time, I was also involved in trying to help farm workers get better pay for their work, when one of my associate pastors told me an anecdote he had heard about a scholar so passionate in his search for truth that he would travel the world over in search of truth—however, when the scholar's wife told him that he was treating her unfairly, the wife discovered that the scholar had no interest in that kind of truth. After sharing this anecdote with me, my associate mentioned to me that his salary didn't compare well with my 'senior pastor' salary. Suddenly I realized that I too didn't need to 'search for truth' so much as to rather allow 'truth to find me' and to 'practice what I preach'. I discovered how easily 'self-interests' can powerfully influence one's values, and how easily rationalization can blind us to truth and justice.

I have had difficulty discussing peace and justice issues without using violent language, like 'waging war on terrorism' or 'fighting for peace'. After all, it is 'fighting for peace' that starts wars, and 'redemptive violence' that continues violence. And yet, striving for peace does remain a struggle against opposition. I have often found that, when seeking to overcome poverty, the practice of war, or any injustices, I have been surrounded with a religious tradition that too easily supports a false priestly practice of calling "peace, peace, when there is no peace" rather than a responsible prophetic practice that calls for changes in unjust and oppressive conditions. The 'Middle Ground' in any controversy is not necessarily the 'Common Ground' of responsible values. Those working to overcome poverty have often been accused of conducting a 'Class War' when opposing entrenched interests and oppressive policies, when in fact since the 1980s a real 'Class War' has been waged in America by those interests and policies to reverse the earlier War on Poverty, resulting in a growing gap between rich and poor. Likewise, those working to end militarism have been labeled unpatriotic or unrealistic, when in fact militarism has led to the erosion of democratic values and proven unable to truly provide security. Although using terms such as 'fighting' or 'waging war' is not desirable, seeking to end poverty or ending wars is a partisan effort to overcome a status quo of oppressive structures and entrenched interests defended by those of the "Old Way", requiring a prophetic effort calling for "Living in a New Way."

Thomas Merton struggled with this same issue, and his writings have helped me in dealing with this matter. He wrote:

> "To some, peace merely means the liberty to exploit other people without fear of retaliation or interference...or the freedom to rob one another with out interruption...or the leisure to devour the goods of the earth without being compelled to interrupt their pleasures to feed those whom their greed is starving. And to practically everybody peace simply means the absence of any physical violence that might cast a shadow over lives devoted to the satisfaction of their animal appetites for comfort and pleasure...their idea of peace is only another form of war."

Looking backwards, it may appear that history, being what happened, was inevitable, but Merton believed, like Teilhard de Chardin, that when looking forward the future is open, not closed, depending on our actions.

Driving in North Sacramento recently, I came upon a street called "Peacekeeper Way" which led to McClellan Airport, a former military base. Later, when I asked a friend who had worked there to explain where the term 'Peacekeeper' came from, he enthusiastically told me with great pride that the Peacekeeper was the MX missile, a land-based ICBM that could carry 10 re-entry vehicles, each armed with a 300 kiloton warhead with twenty times the power of the bomb dropped on Hiroshima during World War II. Another person said the Peacekeeper MX Missile had been responsible for the Cold War's success in keeping peace between Russia and the U.S.

Reflecting on this, I see several fallacies. If peace is simply the 'absence of war', perhaps the name 'Peacekeeper' is appropriate. However if peace is a positive term, a holistic term, then it is misnamed. Further, if the Cold War was not a war, but peace, then we were living in Orwell's 'Nineteen Eighty-Four' thesis spelled out in real life: war is peace, war is perpetual, the Ministry of Peace deals with war, and the Ministry of Truth deals with propaganda. Further, if peace is simply whatever is in the interests of the United States, perhaps 'Peacekeeper' was appropriate. But if our Latin American policies worked against the interest of the people of Central America, or if our occupation with troops in Iraq was to guarantee us getting "our oil" that happened to be under their land, or if trade policies or the International Monetary Fund perpetuate the growing gap between the rich and poor nations, or if our missiles in countries surrounding Russia protect "our security" yet threaten "their security", then the 'Peacekeeper' was misnamed, unless it meant Peacekeeping for Americans while threatening everyone else.

'Peacekeeper' assumed that whatever situation existed at the moment was already peace, regardless of unjust conditions or poverty or inequalities. In reality, what was required in that situation was not a 'Peacekeeper', but a 'Peacemaker'—or better yet, a 'Peace Creator'. The reality of living in the 21st Century is that security for one must demand security for all, and that peace for one must be peace for all. There can be no real security for anyone as long as conditions exist that make many people desperate and resentful.

When a colleague had told me early in my journey, "Your trouble, Jerry, is that you want to be a 'prophet' and not a 'pastor'," I at first resented the comment, then after reflecting about it, felt he was probably right. From then on I decided to eagerly seek, not the avoidance or suppression of conflict, but to seek out and confront conflict deliberately, trusting that healing, growth, justice and peace can come out of crisis. At that time I put this decision into words and addressed it to the person to whom I was responsible:

> "In no sense am I satisfied with my ministry to date. I have not actualized the many possibilities lying before me; too often occasions for creative discovery and interpretation of the gospel have been ignored, cries for unleashing the power of redemptive-community have been allowed to be snuffed out by cowardice in

the face of church-as-usual demands by those who have no sight. I've been unable to effectively burst-out in imaginative action and creative leadership, a responsibility I feel called to do in the stewardship of my life. Hell, we've got plenty of mediocrity (and I thank God for the many who diligently carry on keeping wheels turning, machinery oiled...surely they are blessed of God), but dammit, somehow I just can't be content to drift, to win the prizes handed out for those who agree not to rock the boat."

Although I was encouraged by him, and later by others, to try to develop such a ministry, I soon discovered that such a style of peacemaking, at least the way I tried to do it, was often not well accepted. I rejected, and advocated that others in church and society also reject, the use of violence. The use of violence as a tactic may have often in an earlier era served as a successful adaptive mechanism for coping with primitive and hostile environments. In the past, threats to existence were often of a physical nature, and especially in times of emergency resorting to the use of violence in fighting against them may have been effective. In our day, however, the threats and stresses in life are more often social in nature, and violence becomes counter productive.

Therefore, I have tried to affirm a nonviolent, though an aggressive, assertive and confrontational style of dealing with conflicts and injustice in my peacemaking efforts as appropriate in our scientific and technological era. While I believe this has in general been a good decision, my aggressiveness has also at times been a hindrance to my peacemaking efforts. In a society addicted to using violence to deal with conflict and opposition, and for furthering its own greed and self-interest, this should not be surprising. But to be honest, some of this hindering reaction from others is due to my own natural competitiveness, my own egotistical needs, and especially my still lacking ability and commitment to living an authentic Active Nonviolent Life, this New Way of Living. I am sure that every serious peacemaker must struggle to consistently live assertive nonviolent action without losing a contagious love and passion for people. As Thich Nhat Hanh reminds: "Nonviolence does not mean non-action. Nonviolence means we *act* with love and compassion. The moment we stop acting, we undermine the principle of nonviolence."

My journey of peacemaking had led to my trying to do a prophetic ministry. In the 1950s and 60s it seemed as though social movements were beginning to bring significant improvements in race and poverty issues. However the doors quickly closed. Many of the movements continued for some time, although the assassinations of Martin L. King Jr. and Bobby Kennedy were simply the foretaste that hopes for these changes would not be soon realized. Every effort was made to conceal our failure in Vietnam, but an honest accounting of it has to recognize that the war had been for us one of choice, not necessity, and entered into as our American attempt to salvage as best we could the ending colonial era in the interest of extending our own power. The lesson we ought to have learned from that war was that new opportunities were opening for us to establish new relationships with the rest of the world, especially to the newly developing world, built on mutual trust that justice and peace would be in everyone's self-interest. If we had learned that lesson it would have been victory, having learned that 'there is no way to peace, peace is the way". Instead, the Cold War and the arms race continued, and the social movements for change ground to a snail's pace.

I had been part of a generation that believed victory came from winning wars, especially the Great War, the Good War, World War II. Many people still believe that today. The truth is that the only thing that could possibly have made it a good war was if it had led us to keeping General MacArthur's pledge "to preserve in peace what we had won in war." But trying to "preserve Peace" through a culture of military power and developing a military/industrial complex and opposing Vietnamese aspirations for independence by continuing colonial era policies, was bound to fail. There is no way to 'preserve' a false peace, even as 'there is no way to peace, peace is the way'. For peace is an organic, living, dynamic, always changing set of relationships requiring constant review and a balancing that cannot exclude anyone.

Later there were times I had hopes that major changes were occurring—the Sanctuary movement in the 1970s, Nuclear disarmament in the '80s, Feminism along the way, Liberation Theology, Small Base Communities, Political reform, even Progressive Theological thought, etc.—and yet important as these movements were, they were not strong enough to defer America's reliance on following the Old Ways. The abiding faith of too many Americans in the 1980s and into the new century was Victory through Strength, Peace in a Culture of Violence, trust in a Trickle Down Economy, and justifying privileges for the rich and powerful that revealed the true soul and spirituality of political leadership in our country. I had gone the Civil Disobedience route, being arrested, paying the price as disrupter of the peace—really, not peace all, but the sickness of non-engagement—and had been satisfied to keep working for positive change even though experiences of failure and defeat kept occurring, in the certainty that some time in the future, if not tomorrow, surely within the next years, or decades, or eventually, the fruit of faithful action would be rewarded in a new society. I took some comfort in believing that the Kingdom of God is already operational among us and within us, and a present reality in the world while still incomplete, the "already but not yet" idea. However, if our prayer is "Thy Kingdom Come on Earth as in Heaven" we are committed to continue working and expecting to see real change for peace and justice here and now.

Each Memorial Day we are reminded in messages that more than a million of our military have died fighting for our freedom, that war is honorable, that those going to war are doing a most honorable thing, and that love of country is best expressed by people who are ready to militarily fight for their country. In fact, the million who have died does not include the many more millions of foreign military that died, or the far greater number of non-combatants that have died in wars, especially non-Americans, and especially during the last 70 years when wars killed a far larger number of civilians than military personnel, since aerial bombing, atomic bombs, and smart bombs allow killing even of those who cannot be seen. Even more, it does not include the many more who suffer and die because as General/President Eisenhower said: "Every gun made, every warship launched, signifies in the final sense, a theft from those who hunger and are not fed, those who are cold and are not clothed." Obviously, war is a horrible way to solve problems and conflicts. Surely a better way must be found. Until we reject our commitment to 'Redemptive Violence' we will never solve the problems in our local communities, in our nation, or in the world, whether poverty, health care, education, environmental issues, or anything else, especially peace and justice.

War and militarism is the elephant in the room, and until we reject Redemptive Violence we will continue short-changing all other issues. War is the most obvious example of Redemptive Violence, and during my lifetime we have given it our highest priorities. It has cost us monetarily many billions of dollars, and will continue costing many more billions in coming years, and it has forfeited our claim to be an honorable and peaceful nation. We Americans must demand that this addiction to war and our trust in Redemptive Violence must change. For any person of spiritual faith, and especially for those who call themselves Christian, this is scandalous. Martin Luther King, Jr. reminded us: "He who passively accepts evil is as much involved in it as he who helps to perpetrate it. He who accepts evil without protesting against it is really cooperating with it." Violence is the problem. To believe it is 'Redemptive' is immoral. It is time to reject our trust in Redemptive Violence and respond with a full commitment to Active Nonviolence.

Walter Wink has documented how the Myth of Redemptive Violence is the dominant myth in our lives, how it has been socialized in our children in their process of maturation, and continues into our adulthood. The American media consistently undergirds the Myth. He uses the cartoon character Popeye as an example of how Redemptive Violence is even basic to our comics. The brute Bluto abuses Olive Oyl, Popeye's girlfriend, and Popeye tries to stop him and suffers violent mauling from Bluto, until finally Popeye downs a can of spinach, and then is able to demolish the villain to heroically save Olive Oyl and be hailed as the hero. Popeye's violence is seen as redemptive. The process never varies. They never discuss the matter to explore or learn a better way to settle the problem. Likewise, in the movies, Westerns evidence the same process: a conflict develops, fighting begins and after the white hats, the good guys, have been nearly defeated, they finally always rally to defeat the black hats, the bad guys, to save the day, restore order and justice, and usually win the beautiful girl. Again, Redemptive Violence prevails.

By the time the average child is old enough to vote, they have viewed 15,000 murders, 36,000 hours of TV and have been effectively socialized into a culture of violence by a media that has made violence entertaining and exciting, and assured that the Myth of Redemptive Violence had been indoctrinated as the ultimate solution to personal and social conflict. Violence is seen as good and justifiable as long as 'good' people destroy 'bad' people.

The belief and practice of Redemptive Violence is as ancient as the pyramids or as modern as the latest death in the electric chair. It is the father whipping his boy to teach him to be a good boy, the white red-necked mob lynching the Negro slave, the state electrocuting a murderer, or a nation warring on another nation trying to stop terrorists. It is the belief in the power of violence to bring peace. In the Old Testament, Redemptive Violence was the rationalization that it was Yahweh's will to kill all the inhabitants and destroy the cities as they conquered them, a belief some still cling to today, and has led to the terrible consequence today of blocking peace in the Middle East in the Israel/Palestine situation. For some Christians today, addiction to Redemptive Violence lies behind their understanding of the atonement as the necessity for the violent death of Jesus, who they believe died for their sins as payment of a ransom to a God who demands sacrifice before forgiveness can be given, a belief that denies understanding the God of unconditional love and Grace that is central for so many Christians, and has led today to the terrible consequence of blocking cooperation among all religions working together for peace and justice. And for a small number of fundamentalist Muslims today, it is trust in Redemptive Violence that has led today to the criminal acts of terrorism and male chauvinism advocated as rationalizations that it is Allah's will to kill those who don't follow strict Sharia Law and to dominate women who do, and blocks efforts for a more peaceful and just world. In the U.S. Redemptive Violence offered justification for killing Native Americans and taking Mexican lands, and has led today to our foreign policy that legitimizes acts of self-interest and Empire aspirations. All clear thinking and spiritually inclined Jews, Christians and Muslims, must necessarily reject such rationalizations and misconceptions regarding Redemptive Violence before we can hope to realize our hopes for a more peaceful and just world.

James Carroll in his book 'Constantine's Sword' said that the question that should have been asked of the Nazis was: "How could you have murdered the Jews?" However, he said the question that should have been addressed to the German folk, and especially the German Christians, was rather: "How could you have not cared that the Nazis prepared to murder, and then did murder, millions of Jews in front of you in his attempt at the 'final solution'? Why did you not see that your passivity and indifference had effectively become collaboration?" Likewise, today in America, it is all too easy to blame the atrocity of the Iraq War on President Bush, the Neo-Cons, the political right wing or right wing religious conservatives for the fears that followed 9/11. However, the proper question to be addressed to those just mentioned, and really to all of us as well, should be: "How could we have not cared, and why did we not see, that our passivity and indifference became collaboration in the militarization of our country, and in justifying the sacredness of war itself by our belief and practice of Redemptive Violence that underlies our entire culture?"

The Nuremberg War Crime Tribunal, 1950, following World War II, which the United States strongly encouraged, plainly stated: "Individuals have international duties which transcend the national obligations of obedience. Therefore (individual citizens) have the duty to (refuse to obey) domestic laws to prevent crimes against peace and humanity from occurring." In the midst of his civil rights marches, Martin Luther King, Jr. told us: "He who passively accepts evil is as much involved in it as he who helps to perpetrate it." Gandhi had told us: "You assist an evil system most effectively by obeying its orders and decrees. An evil system never deserves such allegiance. Allegiance to it means partaking of the evil. A good person will resist an evil system with his or her whole soul." In the midst of the oppression in El Salvador in 1978, Bishop Oscar Romero proclaimed: "A church that does not provoke any crisis, preach a gospel that does not unsettle, proclaim a word of God that does not get under anyone's skin, or a word of God that does not touch the real sin of the society in which it is being proclaimed: what kind of gospel is that?" Yet, in America today, five years into a totally unjust war in Iraq, our President and Congress, the media and general public, and even the majority of churches, fail to denounce and oppose the killing, violence, torture, lying, and dishonor of this crime against peace and humanity.

The turmoil in the world today is evidence that our old systems operating in domestic and international relations are dysfunctional. The old systems ought to die—and in fact, the chaos is indication that they are in fact dying. Though new systems have not yet been born, birth-pang signs of the new are all around us. I realize that too much of my energy that is needed to bring positive change has been co-opted in fighting the old systems that are no longer adequate. Fighting against the old ways saps one's energy in the nearly hopeless task of dragging along those too timid to let go of the failing past, and even more, fighting to overcome the resistance of those benefiting from the status quo who want to preserve their privileged positions even though it perpetuates poverty and carnage in a violent world. Gandhi reminded us: "We must be the change we want to see in the world." Instead of using our energy fighting the old ways, we must increasingly use our energies living and building the new ways, trusting that we are only beginning to understand the power of love, even as we are learning the weakness of force and violence.

My entire unfinished journey of peacemaking has seen a continuous struggle between the old and new ways of living. No sooner had I first set off on my journey after the end of WWII than dreams and hopes for new ways experienced the founding of the United Nations and the 'Universal Declaration of Human Rights' based on the sacredness of human life. However, at the same time the old ways were reinforced when the 'International Monetary Fund' and 'World Bank' were established, based on human life as a commodity of exchange, and has continually worked to the advantage of developed nations, and to the detriment of underdeveloped nations. Likewise, a healing and life-giving 'Marshall Plan' was countered at the same time by a destructive and life-threatening Cold War.

I had to learn that even as the sunrise only slowly lightens the sky before finally overcoming the darkness of night, even so are oppression and injustice finally overcome. Only gradually does the morning light dispel the darkness. Justice William O. Douglass, the crusader for justice, reminded us that we must not become impatient, that darkness capitulates slowly, but that we must rather act boldly and confident that change will come, however slowly, lest we become discouraged as victims of the darkness. I had to learn from Pere Teilhard de Chardin that anticipation of the grandeur of sunrise is a source of energy we need to continue the struggle of peacemaking.

Our nation's founding fathers had a dream, and they adopted a Constitution aiming to fulfill it. It was a good Constitution, and yet fell short of perfection in many respects, requiring Amendments to make it available for citizens owning no property, and for slaves, women and others who had been left out, amendments which only came after intense struggles to overcome the resistance of those who either lacked the founders' vision or selfishly sought to protect their interests in the status quo.

Likewise, the prophets and dreamers of peace have suffered rejection, and too often crucifixion or assassination. Prophets have always been dreamers, from the old ones who dreamt of "lions and lambs lying down together", of "swords being turned into plows", and of "a new heaven and a new earth", to our later day prophets who have dreamt of "if you build it they will come", of General MacArthur's "to preserve in peace what we have won in war", of John Kennedy's "quest for peace", and King's "I have a Dream". None of these dreams have been fully realized, but each dream first inspired its dreamer and then inspired many others to get to work to make their dream come true. Dreams of a peaceful world, a world without violence, a world without war, may seem idealistic and hopelessly unrealistic, but it is not the dream of peace that is unrealistic, but rather, the acceptance of war and violence as acceptable solutions to the conflicts on our planet that is totally unrealistic. Cesar Chavez was insightful when he said: "We are only beginning to understand the power of love because we are just beginning to understand the weakness of force and oppression." Therefore, it is good that we continue to dream and pray for peace, while realizing that it is time we accept the responsibility and sacred task to manage the world for achieving it.

Hence, on September 2, 2008, exactly 63 years since I witnessed the end of World War II as an Honor Guard aboard the USS Missouri in Japan when General MacArthur signed the Surrender and Peace Document, as I sit here looking out at the sunrise over Yosemite Valley from Glacier Point, I am filled with hope for the future. I am hopeful, though not optimistic.

I am hopeful for many reasons. I am hopeful because the different religions of the world, which too often in the past have contributed to a divided world, are increasingly recognizing their shared common values and spirituality and respecting and honoring one another. I am hopeful because science and technology and globalization have enabled us to be able to eradicate hunger and poverty, and provide basic healthcare and essential material necessities for all people of the earth. I am hopeful because we have awakened to the threats of ecological disaster, global warming and exploding populations and are beginning to understand how to respond to them in positive ways. I am hopeful because increasingly we are recognizing that we live in One World, on one earth, that nations must serve the common good, that each nation needs to find its proper relationship to the whole, and that an effective United Nations is essential for the common good and for our very survival. I am hopeful because today we know that conflict doesn't necessarily need to end in violence, and that nonviolent alternatives can lead to creative and desirable solutions. I am hopeful because honesty requires that we reject the belief that there can be such a thing as Redemptive Violence, as individuals in all cultures and religions are increasingly learning the power of Active Nonviolence, and as Peace and Justice Movements around the world have effectively demonstrated through the power of nonviolent actions that "there is no way to peace, peace is the way."

I am hopeful, if not optimistic. As President Vaclav Havel of Czechoslovakia said: "Hope is not the conviction that something will turn out well, but the certainty that something makes sense regardless of how it turns out." He reminded us that optimism can too easily be a lazy anticipation that things will turn out well and be an inevitable success, without necessitating a firm commitment to working to make it happen. We all know that each of the hopes stated in the preceding paragraph can, and will be, opposed and contested in the continuing struggle between the Old and New Way of Living.

That struggle will take place within each individual, within each nation, within each culture and religion, and within our One World struggling to recognize we are a united world. The dynamics of this struggle can easily lead to chaos and the defeat of our hopes. However, the power of love and active nonviolent relationships can enable the dynamics of this struggle to lead to the fulfillment of the dreams of the prophets. I am hopeful for the future in my journey of peacemaking, knowing that hopes for future peace requires the willingness to work to make it happen, and the willingness to work for it because it makes sense regardless of its chances for success, simply because it is good.

EPILOGUE

THIS JOURNEY REMAINS UNFINISHED.

In the Presidential Election Campaign taking place September 2008, we can clearly see the struggle between the Old and New Way of Living.

Is our War on Terrorism an effective way to deal with the threat of terrorism? If terrorists are those who threaten others, is our nation then acting as a terrorist nation? Should we have started this war in Iraq? Should the bottom line in Health Care be profitability for Health Insurers and Pharmaceutical Companies or the health and wellbeing of people? Should solving global warming be allowed to influence our private lifestyles? Does the Common Good have any claim on individual rights? If trade agreements benefit our nation yet work to the disadvantage of poorer nations, should they be continued? Is it right to deny other nations the right to develop and possess nuclear weapons, when we justify possession of them for ourselves? When we claim a right to make pre-emptive war when we perceive a possible threat to our security, can we deny that right for others? Do Family Values refer to personal values only, or do they also refer to structures of a society itself?

How we respond to these issues, and dozens of others, will determine whether our nation is mired in destructive ways of Old, or attempting to enter new creative, sustainable, and healing ways. Although both political candidates nod to some New Ways, it is the Obama campaign that most often challenges Old Ways and advocates possible New directions for the future, while the opposition appears to be confident that tidying up the Old Ways would be sufficient.

The real test, however, will face whoever wins the election, when the military/industrial complex that President/General Dwight D. Eisenhower warned of nearly 50 years ago, who together with the financial and pharmaceutical and other self-interest lobbyists and corporations that have become the invisible government and real Power today, will seek to control Congress, and the public through their growing control of financial might and the media, so as to continue the Old Ways that profit the few.

Yet, I can remain hopeful, because as Bill Coffin, a former university minister friend of mine, said: "Hope planted in a hopeless situation changes the situation." And I.F. Stone's words have often sustained me: "The only kinds of fights worth fighting are those you are going to lose, because somebody has to fight them and lose and lose and lose until someday, somebody who believes as we do wins. For somebody to win an important major fight a hundred years hence, a lot of other people have to be willing—for the sheer fun and joy of it—to go right ahead and fight, knowing they're going to lose". Many people have been persevering a long time for a peaceful world. Indeed, the civil rights and human rights movements, the solidarity and global justice organizing, and global environmental awareness, all continue on this journey of achieving peace for the world. Richard Deats, former executive director of Fellowship of Reconciliation, often reminded us: "Gandhi never ceased stressing the power of the indomitable will that refuses to be defeated."

Yes, this journey remains unfinished and has been a long road leading me to the difficult truth that there is no other way to peace than 'the way of peace'- a deeply proactive nonviolent loving engagement with the world.

From my outlook at Glacier Point, I am again presented with the pervasive immense and awesome beauty of life. Feeling the warmth of the sun rising, I turn with the Earth to welcome a new day in the spirit of prayer, acknowledging many others who have preceded me and shared in this Unfinished Journey, and inviting others to join in the journey of peacemaking.

Eternal One—we cannot see or touch you, but you are more real than all we can see or touch. May we, in seeing and touching all that we can, discover your presence. Eternal One— always more than we can ever understand, yet we sense your presence in every good thing, in every human face, in each new light of day, even in the darkness of night. We glimpse your presence in the smile of a child, in the caress of our love mates, in the laughter of friends, in Bread and Wine, even in the faces of our enemies, and in the midst of life in every way. May we live always in your presence. When we search for you, teach us to look forward, not backward. We have asked you in the past to administer the world. Has our time come for us to take on responsibility in managing the world? Has our time come to continue your creation of the world? Help us remember that no matter how little we have, it is enough— and yet, to remember that no matter how much we have, it is not enough if we continue to live in the Old Way of Living by trusting in Redemptive Violence and uncommitted to the Common Good. Help us remember to live in the New Way of Living taught by the prophets of many religions, and especially by our brother Jesus who showed us how to relate to power, money, race, war, and violence in a New Way. Help us remember that, as we abandon violence as a means of coping with conflict, we are holding in our hands not only the fate of humanity, but the fate and fortunes of the universe itself. Help us to live in the Way, the New Way, knowing there is no other way to peace than the way of peace. Keep our faces turned towards this renewal of hope and the grandeur of a new sunrise.

> **"It remains an unfinished journey, both a lifelong spiritual journey and an unending earthly task, trying to cultivate our own nonviolent living, trying to create nonviolent communities, trying to contribute to a nonviolent world, often failing, but having begun—confident that the beckoning dream, the as-yet-unfulfilled quest, and the unconditional hope of peace is not futile—knowing there is no other way to Peace, Peace is the Way."**

—Jerry Pedersen

One World, One People, One Peace.
(Image courtesy of NASA and Visible Earth)

ABOUT THE AUTHOR

THE REV. DR. GERALD O. (Jerry) Pedersen is a retired Lutheran pastor having served in ecumenical campus ministries at University of East Africa, Portland State University, San Francisco State University, Stanford (interim) and as Senior Pastor for a large growing Orange County congregation. He holds a doctorate in theology with post-doctoral work at London School of Economics.

It was while serving aboard the USS Missouri during the Hiroshima and Nagasaki atomic bombings and as Honor Guard at the Japanese Surrender Ceremony that he first committed himself to be a 'peacemaker', challenged by General MacArthur's words at the Surrender Signing, and then, through his interactions with Martin Luther King, Jr. and Cesar Chavez and their lives in pursuing social justice grounded in the 'Nonviolent Action' legacies of Jesus, and Gandhi. These prophets together with other powerful thinkers of his time, and the intensely life-affirming writings of Teilhard de Chardin, Paul Tillich, Walter Wink, Jim Wallis, Thich Nhat Hanh, Father Colman McCarthy, Richard Deats, and others have sustained his relentless optimism and dedication.

Throwing himself into a rich array of life experiences Dr. Pedersen has across-the-board, applied peacemaking in powerfully unique and deeply thoughtful ways. His boundless energies and creativity have marked his every endeavor. With this writing project he hopes to inspire, energize, motivate and support the many others already engaged in creating a more loving, just and peaceful world, and others looking for guidance and encouragement to join in this journey. These times more than ever, call for deep thinking and concerted actions to guide the course of human history to the benefit of our one family and this one Earth.

Jerry and his wife Dru, now live in California's state capitol where he continues with peacemaking alternatives for the 21st century.